LEWIS MUMFORD

THE FUTURE OF TECHNICS & CIVILIZATION

With an Introduction
by COLIN WARD

FREEDOM PRESS
LONDON
1986

Published by
FREEDOM PRESS
in Angel Alley
84B Whitechapel High St
London E1 7QX
1986

ISBN 0 900 384 328

PRINTED IN GT. BRITAIN BY ALDGATE PRESS, LONDON E1

THE FUTURE OF TECHNICS & CIVILIZATION

CONTENTS

INTRODUCTION

"Lewis Mumford is an unusual man. He is not an engineer or a scientist, he isn't an historian or sociologist, you can't identify him as a business man or a literary man or an academic. He seems beyond all those roles. This made him especially attractive to me when I was 19 because his style smelled of the place I wanted to go. He is profound, poetic, knowledgeable. He takes care of the large and small things in his books. *Technics and Civilization* is a good book to start with; if you like it, there are many others of his to turn to. . . ."

— Steve Baer in *The Next Whole Earth Catalog* 1980

In 1948 I wrote to ask Lewis Mumford to contribute an introduction to a new edition of Kropotkin's *Mutual Aid* that Freedom Press proposed to publish. He was working at the time on the first draft of the book that became *The Conduct of Life*, but promised the introduction, saying, "I shall be very proud to have any thing of mine appear under the imprint of a press that Kropotkin helped to found." Alas, the new edition has never — so far — appeared, and Mumford's contribution was never written.

Nearly forty years have passed. The press Kropotkin helped to found celebrates its centenary in 1986 and Lewis Mumford has celebrated his ninetieth birthday. It's a nice mutual compliment that Freedom Press should, with his kind permission, reprint one of the classic Mumford texts. This is the second half of his book *Technics and Civilization*, originally published in 1934, a remarkably original study of the relationship between men and their technology. The inspiration for this book and the sequence that followed it was the Scottish biologist Patrick Geddes, a brilliant systematising mind whose own books scarcely did justice to the range of his thought. Adapting the language of archaeology, Geddes had defined two contrasting phases of industrial civilisation as *paleotechnic* and *neotechnic*. But in Mumford's view he neglected that phase in human history that preceded both, "the

3

important period of preparation, when all the key inventions were either invented or foreshadowed".

To this "dawn age of modern technics" Mumford gave the label *eotechnic,* and he explains that "speaking in terms of power and characteristic materials, the eotechnic phase is a water-and-wood complex, the paleotechnic phase is a coal-and-iron complex, and the neotechnic phase is an electricity-and-alloy complex". The first half of *Technics and Civilization* is a history of European civilisation in terms of the social, political and cultural responses to these phases of technology. These phases do not follow in any crude or mutually exclusive way: they co-exist, overlap and inter-penetrate. If we look around the rooms in which I am writing and you are reading, we will see that the table and chairs are likely to be eotechnic, the stove paleotechnic and the television neotechnic or even produced by technologies which scarcely existed when Mumford was writing, but that the energy sources that produced them are a mixture of all three phases. But what of the *people* that produced them?

The second half of the book, before you now, examines the modern world's responses to the wealth of technologies upon which it depends. Mumford asks, "Can one distinguish and define the specific properties that distinguish it morally, socially, politically, aesthetically from the cruder forms that preceded it? Let us make the attempt."

The reader might be tempted to ask whether the best guide to this attempt is a book written over fifty years ago, at the height of the American Great Depression of the 1930s, when the pace of change in technology has so accelerated since this book was written. What about automation, the new synthetic materials, the silicon chip and micro-electronics, and what about atomic energy and the dilemmas it poses? There are two answers to this question. The first is that human dilemmas do not change. William Morris, for example, tackled the same issues a century ago, back in the paleotechnic era of iron and steam, and his response was much like Mumford's. He said: "The wonderful machines which in the hands of just and far-seeing men would have been used to minimize repulsive labour and to give pleasure — or in other words, added life — to the human race, have been so used on the contrary that they have driven all men into mere frantic haste and hurry, thereby destroying pleasure, that is life, on all hands. They have instead of lightening the labour of workmen, intensified it, and thereby added more weariness yet to the burden which the poor have to carry."[1] In Morris's view, reinforced by Mumford, "It is right and necessary that all men should have work to do which shall be worth doing and be of itself pleasant to do, and which should be done under such conditions as would make it neither over-wearisome nor over-anxious."

The second answer is that Mumford does in fact anticipate many of our contemporary discussions, and raises issues which are seldom discussed all these years later. In the section of his book called "Work for Automaton and Amateur" he remarks:

"Our disregard for the quality of work itself, for work as a vital and educational process, is so habitual that it scarcely ever enters into our social demands. Yet it is plain that in the decision as to whether to build a bridge or a tunnel there is a human question that should outweigh the question of cheapness or mechanical feasibility: namely the number of lives that will be lost in the actual building or the advisability of condemning a certain number of men to spend their entire working days underground supervising tunnel traffic. . . . Similarly the social choice between silk and rayon is not one that can be made simply on the different costs of production, or the difference in quality between the fibres themselves: there also remains, to be integrated in the decision, the question as to difference in working-pleasure between tending silkworms and assisting in rayon production. What the product contributes to the labourer is just as important as what the worker contributes to the product. A well-managed society might alter the process of motor car assemblage, at some loss of speed and cheapness, in order to produce a more interesting routine for the worker. . ".

It might also find that it had a more durable product. The significant thing is that Mumford was identifying issues which are important today and will be in the future. To take his final point about motor car production. As though to support the argument

Mumford was using in the 1930s, a great deal of publicity attended the announced intention of the Volvo car firm in Sweden in the 1970s to abandon the assembly line in favour of small working groups. Let us listen to the comments, not of the journalists, but of Pehr Gyllenhammar, chief executive of the Volvo firm. He says:

"In my opinion any organization in the future must be designed to include the employees as partners. It is a fact that management is not laid off or made to work short hours; it is always the work-force. In Western societies human beings are being more highly educated and at increasing costs to acquire more knowledge, but they are then employed to do less. . . . Today we seem to be faced with the problems of employing people who do not care about their jobs or who plainly dislike their work. This is shown when they leave for an alternative job if they have the option, or when they are absent from their work because it gives them problems of one sort or another. . . . When I joined Volvo in 1971 I was already concerned about the high turnover in staff and absenteeism. This is to be expected in a wealthy society always asking for more, and with jobs made even simpler and more monotonous for the sake of greater efficiency. . . . I insisted on moving away from conveyor belts towards a more flexible carrier system not only because that would increase the degree of freedom of the worker but because it would also have a visual symbolic effect. . . .

"It should be stated from the outset that the vision of a completely different kind of automobile assembly plant did *not* become a reality at Kalmar. Originally the idea was to have a car completed in a small workshop with a few work stations and with some twenty people being responsible for producing a certain quantity of cars. They would be able to complete the whole vehicle and also to identify their vehicles once they were out on the road by being responsible for certain models and certain colours. This concept turned the traditional way of building cars completely upside down because it demanded a material flow to be directed to one spot rather than the product moving on a conveyor-belt in a warehouse where the components were taken off the shelves and the workers were running after the product. We could not solve all the problems of such a radically new concept and settled for a solution where a number of groups were each responsible for a sub-system or a sub-function in a car. . . . The design of the plant should thus make possible the incorporation of small workshops within the big plant."[2]

The Volvo boss was struggling managerially with the challenge Mumford raised theoretically, the problem of turning modern industrial production into "attractive work" as Camillo Berneri put it in an important essay.[3] This is not by any means a problem confined to those countries where the dominant ideology is capitalism. The experience of those countries where the imposed ideology is that of communism suggests that it is even more urgent there.[4]

Mumford could hardly be expected, in 1934, to anticipate our worries about nuclear energy, and yet in a way he does, simply through drawing attention to the existence of renewable sources of energy to replace dependence upon fossil fuels. He wrote: "Apart from the doubtful possibility of harnessing inter-atomic energy, there is the much nearer one of utilizing the sun's energy directly in sun-converters or of utilizing the difference in temperature between the lower depths and the surface of the tropical seas; there is likewise the possibility of applying on a wide scale new types of wind turbine, like the rotor. . . ." Similarly in his discussion of the neotechnic phase in energy generation, he remarks that "because of the enormous vested interest in coal measures, the cheaper sources of energy have not received sufficient systematic attention upon the part of inventors . . .".

No one writing for the general public was introducing such topics in those days. They are the product of a mind habitually on the alert for what we would now call ecologically viable solutions. It is hard to think of another American writer this century (apart from Paul Goodman who addressed himself to the same issues in a more idiosyncratic way) who has so continually interpreted for his fellow citizens fundamental questions that so seldom get asked, let alone answered. Mumford has pursued a long-term plan of books intended to cover those themes he considered important.

Technics and Civilization was intended to be the first volume of a trio of books to which Mumford subsequently gave the collective title "The Renewal of Life". It was followed in 1938 with *The Culture of Cities*, the culmination of his many years' advocacy of a decentralist, regionalist approach to town and country planning, and in 1944 by *The Condition of Man*. His urge to make sense of human history obliged him to add a fourth volume in 1951, and then, in a way, to begin the whole exercise once more with first *The Transformations of Man* in 1955, followed by *The City in History* in 1961, a rewritten version of *The Culture of Cities*, and *The Myth of the Machine* in 1967, which in some ways is an extended prelude to his earlier history of technology, and finally *The Pentagon of Power* in 1970, as a sermon on the way human values had been supplanted by the "megamachine" of modern government.

His book *The Myth of the Machine* is not by any means a rewriting of *Technics and Civilization*. It is much more a further pushing back of the history of technology into pre-history: into the paleolithic and neolithic periods. He claims:

"At every stage man's inventions and transformations were less for the purpose of increasing the food supply or controlling nature than for utilizing his own immense organic resources and expressing his latent potentialities, in order to fulfill more adequately his super-organic demands and aspirations. . . . To consider man, then, as primarily a tool-using animal, is to overlook the main chapters of human history. Opposed to this petrified notion, I shall develop the view that man is pre-eminently a mind-making, self-mastering, and self-designing animal; and the primary locus of all his activities lies first in his own organism, and in the social organisation through which it finds fuller expression."

Such bold assertions illustrate the enormous virtue of Mumford as thinker and writer: he takes his readers seriously and expects them to make the effort to follow his own attempts to make sense of human history. This was nicely illustrated when Theodore Roszak sought to unravel the strands of thought in Mumford's analysis of the evidence. The first of these, he found, was:

"Imaginative reconstructions of the mental processes that may have underlain the inventions and the use of material artifacts we have recovered. This is a style of speculation at which Mumford is the undisputed master. Take, for example, his shrewd recognition of the fact that the chief neolithic crafts — weaving, modelling, pottery-making — are precisely those that modern psychiatry has hit upon as forms of 'occupational therapy' especially capable of restoring emotional balance. This is the sort of insight that illuminates the emotional basis of an entire cultural epoch."[5]

True, of course, but it remains true that the greater part of work in neolithic times, as in our own, has consisted of mindless drudgery. That same 'occupational therapy' might very well consist of a task like assembling the plastic components of ball-point pens or electrical fittings, and it is often held up as an example of the horrors of industrial production that mentally defective people have a better rate of output, with fewer rejects, than normal people undertaking the same task. Yet if you talk to the people involved, their attitudes are entirely different. The patient is proud of his output, and says in as many words, "Look, I have paid my way. You have fed and housed me, but I am self-supporting." The worker asks, "Why have you condemned me to an idiotic task, just because I am obliged to earn a living?" There are dimensions of work that were scarcely considered by Mumford in 1934 and by very few other philosophers since then.

Every kind of work involves routine mechanical tasks, the kind of thing that the blacksmith would delegate to his apprentice, or the executive to one of an army of clerical assistants. The important thing about these chores is the extent to which they are shared, so that they become one among many experiences in a working day or life, and the extent to which the person doing them is part of a larger undertaking. It makes a great deal of difference if we have a personal commitment to this enterprise or not. For example, compare the situation of someone stuffing envelopes for the mailing list of a propagandist venture in, let us say, environment conservation, with that of someone undertaking an identical task as underpaid homework for an enterprise selling the latest kind of anti-dandruff shampoo. Feelings about, and motivations for, the undertaking would be totally different.

Or take the whole field of domestic work, completely unrecognised as work in the official economy simply because it doesn't carry with it a pay entitlement. At the very time when Mumford was writing *Technics and Civilization*, an English author called C. Delisle Burns gave a series of radio talks under the title "Leisure in the Modern World".[6] He was deluged with letters from listeners and one of them was concerned with the revolution in domestic work that had resulted from modern technology. This listener wrote that "going back to my boyhood days — fifty years — the changes in the modern home are almost miraculous", and he listed them under the headings of water, firing, lighting and sanitation, and he explained that "I can remember my father getting the necessary supply of water from a spring by means of buckets with yokes over his shoulders", and that "to get a fire in the morning for the purpose of cooking the food was at times a nightmare, especially when the wood was damp . . . endless blowing with the bellows". As for domestic lighting, he recalled the "farthing dip or rushlight, varied by the ordinary tallow candle" and for sanitation the earth closet with its frequent emptying.

This particular listener remembered that "when I was a boy I was called upon to assist my sister in housework, and it was my job to blacklead the hearth etc. It was the bane of my life. The time taken to get a polish was enormous. . . . Twelve years ago I invested in a dozen stainless knives. This investment proved the greatest of my life. Just think: after every meal the same knives had to be cleaned by means of brickdust and a board."[7]

Here is an important reminder of the significance of such taken-for-granted inventions as stainless steel in ordinary modern life, and it is also a reminder of the items in the domestic economy that he did not mention: the preparation of meals and the disposal of their aftermath, the washing, drying, ironing and disposal of clothes, and the sheer labour of cleaning the house. The mechanization of these tasks, in Mumford's 1934 analysis, "has increased the amount of personal autonomy and personal participation in the household". He is not among those tedious moralists who, secure in the enjoyment of the domestic labour of others themselves, despise other people's preoccupation with household gadgets. But he does warn us that "healthy activity requires restriction, monotony, repetition, as well as change, variety, and expansion".

When the fascinating volume of the correspondence between Lewis Mumford and F. J. Osborn was published,[8] I reviewed it under the heading "The hedgehog and the fox", using the categories that Isaiah Berlin alleges he found in an obscure Greek author who remarked that the fox knows many things while the hedgehog knows one big thing. "Mumford", I said, "as a professional author, has spent his creative years on a series of books which offer a vast synoptic view of human activity. Frederic Osborn, though he too must have written millions of words, is not a professional writer . . . he has spent *his* creative years propagating one big idea — the decentralised new town built on garden city principles — while contriving to earn his living at the same time. Mumford glories in being a fox: he describes himself as a 'generalist', while Osborn has been forced into the hedgehog role by his own sense of priorities: he calls himself a specialist on things in general, and every now and then chafes at the restriction of his spread of activities that this implies." No sooner had these words appeared in print when the telephone rang and there was Osborn, thanking me for my kind words and saying that he had searched in vain for the origin of the aphorism about hedgehogs and foxes, and consequently didn't know whether to purr or growl about my categorization. So I sent him my copy of Berlin's great essay (which is actually about Tolstoy's view of history), and he agreed that while he was undoubtedly a hedgehog yearning to be a fox, his friend Mumford was unquestionably a fox, with an omnivorous diet of the whole range of human wisdom and learning. This has not been good for him. The reason is that during his lifetime the academic world has expanded so enormously that the odious idea has grown up that scholars don't need to be taken seriously unless they work within the "field" or "discipline" in which they are fully paid-up and accredited members. Mumford ranges throughout history and across the boundaries of different kinds of knowledge, so that, as Theodore Roszak admiringly notes, he will take from the Egyptian sixth dynasty an inscription that reads:

"The army returned in safety
After it had hacked up the land of the Sand Dwellers
After it had thrown down its enclosures
After it had cut down its fig trees and vines
After it had cast fire into all its dwellings
After it had killed troops in it by many-thousand"

— and will follow it with the comment, "That sums up the course of Empire everywhere: from the earliest Egyptian palette to the latest American newspaper with its reports, at the moment I write, of the mass atrocities coldbloodedly perpetrated with the aid of napalm bombs and defoliated poisons, by the military forces of the United States on the helpless peasant populations of Vietnam: an innocent people, uprooted, terrorized, poisoned and roasted alive in a futile attempt to make the power fantasies of the American military-industrial-scientific elite 'credible'."[9]

There is no pretence at a spurious academic detachment here. Mumford knows exactly where he stands and why. He is, as the geographer Peter Hall put it, essentially a synthesizer, whose work puts together "most clearly and most passionately" the ideas of others, who never got an adequate hearing themselves. The three figures whose neglected legacy Mumford has done most to promote were Ebenezer Howard, Peter Kropotkin and Patrick Geddes, people so marginal in any academic account of the history of ideas that you could go through a university course in the history of human settlements and not hear a word about any of them. Hall stresses that Mumford borrowed some of his vision from the humble Victorian inventor Howard,[10] but that "More of it, he got from Geddes[11] and Kropotkin. His greatest achievement was to take Geddes' visionary ramblings and to make of them not merely sense, which certainly Geddes never did, but also the inspiration that Geddes so passionately felt but could not adequately convey. To this he added a specially American ingredient, that goes back to Thoreau and Muir and the Southern

Regionalists of the 1920s and 1930s: the notion of ecological balance and the planned husbanding of natural resources."[12]

Mumford's debt to Kropotkin was profound and handsomely acknowledged. In *The City in History* he explains precisely why *Fields, Factories and Workshops*[13] is a more important book today than when it was first written, and I make no apology for quoting his opinion at length:

"Almost half a century in advance of contemporary economic and technical opinion, he had grasped the fact that the flexibility and adaptability of electric communication and electric power, along with the possibilities of intensive, biodynamic farming, had laid the foundations for a more decentralized urban development in small units, responsive to direct human contact, and enjoying both urban and rural advantages. Industry, he saw, was no longer tied to the coalmine, even when coal remained a source of power; nor was it tied to the railroad and the big city: neither efficiency nor economy was to be equated with big units of production. Kropotkin foresaw what many big corporations were to discover only during the Second World War; namely, that even when the total assemblage was a big one, the farming out of special industrial operations in 'bits and pieces' actually often made the reputed economies of concentrated large-scale organization, the industrial tendency that justified other forms of metropolitan bigness, dubious. The finer the technology, the greater the need for the human initiative and skill conserved in the small workshop. Effective transportation and fine organization were often superior to the mere physical massing of plant under one roof.

"Kropotkin realized that the new means of rapid transit and communication, coupled with the transmission of electric power in a network, rather than a one-dimensional line, made the small community on a par in essential technical facilities with the overcongested city. By the same token, rural occupations once isolated and below the economic and cultural level of the city could have the advantages of scientific intelligence, group organization, and animated activities, originally a big city monopoly; and with this the hard and fast division between urban and rural, between industrial worker and farm worker, would break down too. Kropotkin understood these implications before the invention of the motor car, the radio, the motion picture, the television system, and the world-wide telephone — though each of these inventions further confirmed his penetrating diagnosis by equalizing advantages between the central metropolis and the once peripheral and utterly dependent small communities. With the small unit as a basis, he saw the opportunity for a more responsible and responsive local life, with greater scope for the human agents who were neglected and frustrated by mass organizations."[14]

This is the vision of the future of industry that underpins Mumford's text, and of course it has come true in ways that neither he nor Kropotkin envisaged. The world-wide decentralization of industry that Kropotkin foresaw has happened. Britain, which in his day was "the workshop of the world" has become a net importer of manufactured goods, and so, remarkably, has the United States. The great industrial cities have become derelict monuments to the paleotechnic age of iron and steel. Their throbbing heart is not in heavy industry but in their commercial centres and their biggest employer is not manufacturing but the municipal services that keep them going.

Another of Mumford's mentors, Ebenezer Howard, had declared in 1904, "I venture to suggest that while the age in which we live is the age of the great closely-compacted, overcrowded city, there are already signs, for those who can read them, of a coming change so great and so momentous that the twentieth century will be known as the period of the great exodus, the return to the land. . . ."[15] This return to the land has happened, not in the sense of any increase in the agricultural population, which has declined dramatically as the industrialization of farming brought a great increase in production and an equally great reduction of the numbers of employed farm workers. Except for a minority of people (but a growing one as the official economy declines and the "informal sector" increases) the combination of brain work and manual work and of industrial and horticultural employment that Kropotkin, and Mumford, hoped for, has not changed the nature of work.

For two of the expected revolutions of the twentieth century just have not happened in the West, while in the East they have brought results which have been the opposite of popular expectations. They are the revolution in the control of capital and in the disposal of power. Ownership of capital may have been dispersed, but the "commanding heights" of the economy have been concentrated in fewer and fewer hands. Political democracy may bring changes of government as a result of the popular vote, but the power of the state itself has grown immeasurably. This is why Mumford, in his later writings, has moved further and further back in history to examine the nature of power, and find parallels even in neolithic Egypt, remarking in *The Myth of the Machine* that "this essential coalition between royal military power and often dubious supernatural authority anticipated a similar alliance between scientists and mathematical games theorists with the higher agents of government today; and was subject to similar corruptions, miscalculations, and hallucinations". And it is why, in the sequel to that book, *The Pentagon of Power*, he raises once more the key issue of the *control* of technology. While compiling that last important work in his long and continually-related series of books on the key issues of Western civilization, he confided to F. J. Osborn that "the themes I have developed are so well fortified with evidence and because, far from over-stating my case against our runaway technology, I show how much more beneficial its real improvements will be once we get control of the whole system, and use it for our purposes, instead of letting the megamachine use us for *its* purposes. As to the megamachine, the threat that it now offers turns out to be even more frightening, thanks to the computer, than even I in my most pessimistic moments had ever suspected. Once fully installed our whole lives would be in the hands of those who control the system, much as the life of an American conscript is now in the hands of the Pentagon and the White House, and no decision from birth to death would be left to the individual. The joke of the whole business is that this miscarriage of technology has been the ideal goal of almost all utopias . . .".[16]

This is far from the buoyant mood of the text before you now, but the message is the same.

Colin Ward

Notes

1. William Morris "Art and Socialism" Lecture delivered before the Secular Society of Leicester,23 January, 1884. Reprinted in several modern collections of Morris's works.

2. Pehr Gyllenhammar "Design as an expression of company philosophy" Lethaby Lecture, Royal College of Art 10 November 1977. (Royal College of Art, 1980)

3. Camillo Berneri "The problem of work" (1938), reproduced in Vernon Richards (ed) *Why Work?* (Freedom Press 1983)

4. Miklos Haraszti *A Worker in a Worker's State* (Penguin 1977)

5. Theodore Roszak "Scholar, Poet, Prophet" (*Manas*, Los Angeles, 31 January 1968)

6. C. Delisle Burns *Leisure in the Modern World* (Allen and Unwin 1932)

7. Listener's letter included in appendix to Burns *op cit*

8. *Michael Hughes (ed) The Letters of Lewis Mumford and Frederic J. Osborn (Adams and Dart 1971)*

9. *Lewis Mumford The Myth of the Machine* (Harcourt, Brace 1967)

10. Ebenezer Howard *Garden Cities of Tomorrow*, edited by F. J. Osborn with an introductory essay by Lewis Mumford (Faber 1946)

11. Of the various books about Geddes the reader is likely to encounter the best are Paddy Kitchen *A Most Unsettling Person* (Gollancz 1975) and Philip Boardman *The Worlds of Patrick Geddes* (Routledge 1978)

12. Peter Hall "The Neotechnic Vision" (*Built Environment* Vol 8 No 4, 1982)

13. Peter Kropotkin *Fields, Factories and Workshops* (1898, new edition Freedom Press 1985)

14. Lewis Mumford *The City in History* (Secker and Warburg 1961)

15. Ebenezer Howard, opening the discussion of a paper on "Civics as Applied Sociology" by Patrick Geddes, read at a meeting in the London School of Economics and Political Science, 18 July 1904, reprinted in Helen Meller *The Ideal City* (Leicester University Press 1979)

16. Mumford to Osborn 31 July 1968 in Michael Hughes *op cit*

I
COMPENSATIONS AND REVERSIONS

1: Summary of Social Reactions

Each of the three phases of machine civilization has left its deposits in society. Each has changed the landscape, altered the physical layout of cities, used certain resources and spurned others, favored certain types of commodity and certain paths of activity, and modified the common technical heritage. It is the sum total of these phases, confused, jumbled, contradictory, cancelling out as well as adding to their forces that constitutes our present mechanical civilization. Some aspects of this civilization are in complete decay; some are alive but neglected in thought; still others are at the earliest stages of development. To call this complicated inheritance the Power Age or the Machine Age is to conceal more facts about it than one reveals. If the machine appears to dominate life today, it is only because society is even more disrupted than it was in the seventeenth century.

But along with the positive transformations of the environment by means of the machine have come the reactions of society against the machine. Despite the long period of cultural preparation, the machine encountered inertia and resistance: in general, the Catholic countries were slower to accept it than were the Protestant countries, and the agricultural regions assimilated it far less completely than the mining districts. Modes of life essentially hostile to the machine have remained in existence: the institutional life of the churches, while often subservient to capitalism, has remained foreign to the naturalistic and mechanistic interests which helped develop the machine. Hence the machine itself has been deflected or metamorphosed to a certain degree by the human reactions which it has set up, or to which, in one manner or another, it has been forced to adapt itself. Many social adjustments have resulted from the machine which were far from the minds of the original philosophers of industrialism. They expected the old social institutions of feudalism to be dissolved by the new order: they did not anticipate that they might be re-crystallized.

It is only in economic textbooks, moreover, that the Economic Man and the Machine Age have ever maintained the purity of their ideal images. Before the paleotechnic period was well under way their images were already tarnished: free competition was curbed from the start by the trade agreements and anti-union collaborations of the very industrialists who shouted most loudly for it. And the retreat from the machine, headed by philosophers and poets and artists, appeared at the very moment that the forces of utilitarianism seemed most coherent and confident. The successes of mechanism only increased the awareness of values not included in a mechanistic ideology—values derived, not from the machine, but from other provinces of life. Any just appreciation of the machine's contribution to civilization must reckon with these resistances and compensations.

2: The Mechanical Routine

Let the reader examine for himself the part played by mechanical routine and mechanical apparatus in his day, from the alarm-clock that wakes him to the radio program that puts him to sleep. Instead of adding to his burden by re-capitulating it, I purpose to summarize the results of his investigations, and analyze the consequences.

The first characteristic of modern machine civilization is its temporal regularity. From the moment of waking, the rhythm of the day is punctuated by the clock. Irrespective of strain or fatigue, despite reluctance or apathy, the household rises close to its set hour. Tardiness in rising is penalized by extra haste in eating breakfast or in walking to catch the train: in the long run, it may even mean the loss of a job or of advancement in business. Breakfast, lunch, dinner, occur at regular hours and are of definitely limited duration: a million people perform these functions within a very narrow band of time, and only minor provisions are made for those who would have food outside this regular schedule. As the scale of industrial organization grows, the punctuality and regularity of the mechanical régime tend to increase with it: the time-clock enters automatically to regulate the entrance and exit of the worker, while an irregular worker—tempted by the trout in spring streams or ducks on salt meadows—finds that these impulses are as unfavorably treated as habitual drunkenness: if he would retain them, he must remain attached to the less routinized provinces of agriculture. "The refractory tempers of work-people accustomed to irregular paroxysms of diligence," of which Ure wrote a century ago with such pious horror, have indeed been tamed.

Under capitalism time-keeping is not merely a means of co-ordinating and inter-relating complicated functions: it is also like money an independent commodity with a value of its own. The school teacher, the lawyer, even the doctor with his schedule of operations conform their functions to a time-table almost as rigorous as that of the locomotive engineer. In the case of child-birth, patience rather than instrumentation is one of the chief requirements for a successful normal delivery and one of the major safeguards against infection in a difficult one. Here the mechanical interference of the obstetrician, eager to resume his rounds, has apparently been largely responsible for the current discreditable record of American physicians, utilizing the most sanitary hospital equipment, in comparison with midwives who do not attempt brusquely to hasten the processes of nature. While regularity in certain physical functions, like eating and eliminating, may in fact assist in maintaining health, in other matters, like play, sexual intercourse, and other forms of recreation the strength of the impulse itself is pulsating rather than evenly recurrent: here habits fostered by the clock or the calendar may lead to dullness and decay.

Hence the existence of a machine civilization, completely timed and scheduled and regulated, does not necessarily guarantee maximum efficiency in any sense. Time-keeping establishes a useful point of reference, and is invaluable for co-ordinating diverse groups and functions which lack any other common frame of activity. In the practice of an individual's vocation such regularity may greatly assist concentration and economize effort. But to make it arbitrarily rule over human functions is to reduce existence itself to mere time-serving and to spread the shades of the prison-house over too large an area of human conduct. The regularity that produces apathy and atrophy—that *acedia* which was the bane of monastic existence, as it is likewise of the army—is as wasteful as the irregularity that produces disorder and confusion. To utilize the accidental, the unpredictable, the fitful is as necessary, even in terms of economy, as to utilize the regular: activities which exclude the operations of chance impulses forfeit some of the advantages of regularity.

In short: mechanical time is not an absolute. And a population trained to keep to a mechanical time routine at whatever sacrifice to health, convenience, and organic felicity may well suffer from the strain of that discipline and find life impossible without the most strenuous compensations. The fact that sexual intercourse in a modern city is limited, for workers in all grades and departments, to the fatigued hours of the day may add to the efficiency of the working life only by a too-heavy sacrifice in personal and organic relations. Not the least of the blessings promised by the shortening of working hours is the opportunity to carry into bodily play the vigor that has hitherto been exhausted in the service of machines.

Next to mechanical regularity, one notes the fact that a good part of the mechanical elements in the day are attempts to counteract the effects of lengthening time and space distances. The refrigeration of eggs, for example, is an effort to space their distribution more uniformly than the hen herself is capable of doing: the pasteurization of milk is an attempt to counteract the effect of the time consumed in completing the chain between the cow and the remote consumer. The accompanying pieces of mechanical apparatus do nothing to improve the product itself: refrigeration merely halts the process of decomposition, while pasteurization actually robs the milk of some of its value as nutriment. Where it is possible to distribute the population closer to the rural centers where milk and butter and green vegetables are grown, the elaborate mechanical apparatus for counteracting time and space distances may to a large degree be diminished.

One might multiply such examples from many departments; they point to a fact about the machine that has not been generally recognized by those quaint apologists for machine-capitalism who look upon every extra expenditure of horsepower and every fresh piece of mechanical apparatus as an automatic net gain in efficiency. In The Instinct of Workmanship Veblen has indeed wondered whether the typewriter, the telephone, and the automobile, though creditable technological achievements "have not wasted more effort and substance than they have saved," whether they are not to be credited with an appreciable economic loss, because they have increased the pace and the volume of correspondence and communication and travel out of all proportion to the real need. And Mr. Bertrand Russell has noted that each improvement in locomotion has increased the area over which people are compelled to move: so that a person who would have had to spend half an hour to walk to work a century ago must still spend half an hour to reach his destination, because the contrivance that would have enabled him to save time had he remained in his original situation now—by driving him to a more distant residential area—effectually cancels out the gain.

One further effect of our closer time co-ordination and our instantaneous communication must be noted here: broken time and broken attention. The difficulties of transport and communication before 1850 automatically acted as a selective screen, which permitted no more stimuli to reach a person than he could handle: a certain urgency was necessary before one received a call from a long distance or was compelled to make a journey oneself: this condition of slow physical locomotion kept intercourse down to a human scale, and under definite control. Nowadays this screen has vanished: the remote is as close as the near: the ephemeral is as emphatic as the durable. While the tempo of the day has been quickened by instantaneous communication the rhythm of the day has been broken: the radio, the telephone, the daily newspaper clamor for attention, and amid the host of stimuli to which people are subjected, it becomes more and more difficult to absorb and cope with any one part of the environment, to say nothing of dealing with it as a whole. The common man is as subject to these interruptions as the scholar or the man of affairs, and even the weekly period of cessation from familiar tasks and contemplative reverie, which was one of the great contributions of Western religion to the discipline of the personal life, has become an ever remoter possibility. These mechanical aids to efficiency and cooperation and intelligence have been mercilessly exploited, through commercial and political pressure: but so far—since unregulated and undisciplined—they have been obstacles to the very ends they affect to further. We have multiplied the mechanical demands without multiplying in any degree our human capacities for registering and reacting intelligently to them. With the successive demands of the outside world so frequent and so imperative, without any respect to their real importance, the inner world becomes progressively meager and formless: instead of active selection there is passive absorption ending in the state happily described by Victor Branford as "addled subjectivity."

3: Purposeless Materialism: Superfluous Power

Growing out of its preoccupation with quantity production is the machine's tendency to center effort exclusively upon the production of material goods. There is a disproportionate emphasis on the physical means of living: people sacrifice time and present enjoyments in order that they acquire a greater abundance of physical means; for there is supposed to be a close relation between well-being and the number of bathtubs, motor cars, and similar machine-made products that one may possess. This tendency, not to satisfy the physical needs of life, but to expand toward an indefinite limit the amount of physical equipment that is applied to living is not exclusively characteristic of the machine, because it has existed as a natural accompaniment of other phases of capitalism in other civilizations. What is typical of the machine is the fact that these ideals, instead of being confined to a class, have been vulgarized and spread—at least as an ideal—in every section of society.

One may define this aspect of the machine as "purposeless materialism." Its particular defect is that it casts a shadow of reproach upon all the non-material interests and occupations of mankind: in particular, it condemns liberal esthetic and intellectual interests because "they serve no useful purpose." One of the blessings of invention, among the naïve advocates of the machine, is that it does away with the need for the imagination: instead of holding a conversation with one's distant friend in reverie, one may pick up a telephone and substitute his voice for one's fantasy. If stirred by an emotion, instead of singing a song or writing a poem, one may turn on a phonograph record. It is no disparagement of either the phonograph or the telephone to suggest that their special functions do not take the place of a dynamic imaginative life, nor does an extra bathroom, however admirably instrumental, take the place of a picture or a flower-garden. The brute fact of the matter is that our civilization is now weighted in favor of the use of mechanical instruments, because the opportunities for commercial production and for the exercise of power lie there: while all the direct human reactions or the personal arts which require a minimum of mechanical paraphernalia are treated as negligible. The habit of producing goods whether they are needed or not, of utilizing inventions whether they are useful or not, of applying power whether it is effective or not pervades almost every department of our present civilization. The result is that whole areas of the personality have been slighted: the telic, rather than the merely adaptive, spheres of conduct exist on sufferance. This pervasive instrumentalism places a handicap upon vital reactions which cannot be closely tied to the machine, and it magnifies the importance of physical goods as symbols—symbols of intelligence and ability and far-sightedness—even as it tends to characterize their absence as a sign of stupidity and failure. And to the extent that this materialism is purposeless, it becomes final: the means are presently converted into an end. If material goods need any other justification, they have it in the fact that the effort to consume them keeps the machines running.

These space-contracting, time-saving, goods-enhancing devices are likewise manifestations of modern power production: and the same paradox holds of power and power-machinery: its economies have been partly cancelled out by increasing the opportunity, indeed the very necessity, for consumption. The situation was put very neatly a long time ago by Babbage, the English mathematician. He relates an experiment performed by a Frenchman, M. Redelet, in which a block of squared stone was taken as the subject for measuring the effort required to move it. It weighed 1080 pounds. In order to drag the stone, roughly chiseled, along the floor of the quarry, it required a force equal to 758 pounds. The same stone dragged over a floor of planks required 652 pounds; on a platform of wood, drawn over a floor of planks, it required 606 pounds. After soaping the two surfaces of wood which slid over each other it required 182 pounds. The same stone was now placed upon rollers three inches in diameter, when it required to put it in motion along the floor of the quarry only 34 pounds, while to drag it by these rollers over a wooden floor it needed but 22 pounds.

This is a simple illustration of the two ways open in applying power to modern production. One is to increase the expenditure of power; the other is to economize in the application of it. Many of our so-called gains in efficiency have consisted, in effect, of using power-machines to apply 758 pounds to work which could be just as efficiently accomplished by careful planning and preparation with an expenditure of 22 pounds: our illusion of superiority is based on the fact that we have had 736 pounds to waste. This fact explains some of the grotesque miscalculations and misappraisals that have been made in comparing the working efficiency of past ages with the present. Some of our technologists have committed the blunder of confusing the increased load of equipment and the increased expenditure of energy with the quantity of effective work done. But the billions of horsepower available in modern production must be balanced off against losses which are even greater than those for which Stuart Chase has made a tangible estimate in his excellent study of The Tragedy of Waste. While a net gain can probably be shown for modern civilization, it is not nearly so great as we have imagined through our habit of looking only at one side of the balance sheet.

The fact is that an elaborate mechanical organization is often a temporary and expensive substitute for an effective social organization or for a sound biological adaptation. The secret of analyzing motions, of harnessing energies, of designing machines was discovered before we began an orderly analysis of modern society and attempted to control the unconscious drift of technic and economic forces. Just as the ingenious mechanical restorations of teeth begun in the nineteenth century anticipated our advance in physiology and nutrition, which will reduce the need for mechanical repair, so many of our other mechanical triumphs are merely stopgaps, to serve society whilst it learns to direct its social institutions, its biological conditions, and its personal aims more effectively. In other words, much of our mechanical apparatus is useful in the same way that a crutch is useful when a leg is injured. Inferior to the normal functioning leg, the crutch assists its user to walk about whilst bone and tissue are being repaired. The common mistake is that of fancying that a society in which everyone is equipped with crutches is thereby more efficient than one in which the majority of people walk on two legs.

We have with considerable cleverness devised mechanical apparatus to counteract the effect of lengthening time and space distances, to increase the amount of power available for performing unnecessary work, and to increase the waste of time attendant upon irrelevant and superficial intercourse. But our success in doing these things has blinded us to the fact that such devices are not by themselves marks of efficiency or of intelligent social effort. Canning and refrigeration as a means of distributing a limited food supply over the year, or of making it available in areas distant from the place originally grown, represent a real gain. The use of canned goods, on the other hand, in country districts when fresh fruits and vegetables are available comes to a vital and social loss. The very fact that mechanization lends itself to large-scale industrial and financial organization, and marches in step with the whole distributing mechanism of capitalist society frequently gives an advantage to such indirect and ultimately more inefficient methods. There is, however, no virtue whatever in eating foods that are years old or that have been transported thousands of miles, when equally good foods are available without going out of the locality. It is a lack of rational distribution that permits this process to go on in our society. Power machines have given a sort of licence to social inefficiency. This licence was tolerated all the more easily because what the community as a whole lost through these misapplied energies enterprising individuals gained in profits.

The point is that efficiency is currently confused with adaptability to large-scale factory production and marketing: that is to say, with fitness for the present methods of commercial exploitation. But in terms of social life, many of the most extravagant advances of the machine have proved to rest on the invention of intricate means of doing things which can be performed at a minor cost by very simple ones. Those complicated pieces of apparatus, first devised by American cartoonists, and later carried onto the stage by comedians like Mr. Joe Cook, in which a whole series of mechanisms and involved motions are created in order to burst a paper bag or lick a postage stamp are not wild products of the American imagination: they are merely transpositions into the realm of the comic of processes which can be witnessed at a hundred different points in actual life. Elaborate antiseptics are offered in expensive mechanically wrapped packages, made tempting by lithographs and printed advertisements, to take the place which common scientific knowledge indicates is amply filled by one of the most common minerals, sodium chloride. Vacuum pumps driven by electric motors are forced into American households for the purpose of cleaning an obsolete form of floor covering, the carpet or the rug, whose appropriateness for use in interiors, if it did not disappear with the caravans where it originated, certainly passed out of existence with rubber heels and steam-heated houses. To count such pathetic examples of waste to the credit of the machine is like counting the rise in the number of constipation remedies a proof of the benefits of leisure.

The third important characteristic of the machine process and machine environment is uniformity, standardization, replaceability. Whereas handicraft, by the very nature of human work, exhibits constant variations and adaptations, and boasts of the fact that no two products are alike, machine work has just the opposite characteristic: it prides itself on the fact that the millionth motor car built to a specific pattern is exactly like the first. Speaking generally, the machine has replaced an unlimited series of variables with a limited number of constants: if the range of possibility is lessened, the area of prediction and control is increased.

And while the uniformity of performance in human beings, pushed beyond a certain point, deadens initiative and lowers the whole tone of the organism, uniformity of performance in machines and standardization of the product works in the opposite direction. The dangers of standardized products have in fact been over-rated by people who have applied the same criterion to machines as they would to the behavior of living beings. This danger has been further over-stressed by those who look upon uniformity as in itself bad, and upon variation as in itself good: whereas monotony (uniformity) and variety are in reality polar characteristics, neither of which can or should be eliminated in the conduct of life. Standardization and repetition have in fact the part in our social economy that habit has in the human organism: by pushing below the level of consciousness certain recurrent elements in our experience, they free attention for the non-mechanical, the unexpected, the personal. (I shall deal with the social and esthetic importance of this fact when I discuss the assimilation of our machine culture.)

4: Co-operation *versus* Slavery

One of the by-products of the development of mechanical devices and mechanical standards has been the nullification of skill: what has taken place here within the factory has also taken place in the final utilization of its products. The safety razor, for example, has changed the operation of shaving from a hazardous one, best left to a trained barber, to a rapid commonplace of the day which even the most inept males can perform. The automobile has transformed engine-driving from the specialized task of the locomotive engineer to the occupation of millions of amateurs. The camera has in part transformed the artful reproductions of the wood engraver to a relatively simple photo-chemical process in which anyone can acquire at least the rudiments. As in manufacture the human function first becomes specialized, then mechanized, and finally automatic or at least semi-automatic.

When the last stage is reached, the function again takes on some

of its original non-specialized character: photography helps reculti-
vate the eye, the telephone the voice, the radio the ear, just as the
motor car has restored some of the manual and operative skills
that the machine was banishing from other departments of existence
at the same time that it has given to the driver a sense of power and
autonomous direction—a feeling of firm command in the midst of
potentially constant danger—that had been taken away from him in
other departments of life by the machine. So, too, mechanization, by
lessening the need for domestic service, has increased the amount
of personal autonomy and personal participation in the household.
In short, mechanization creates new occasions for human effort; and
on the whole the effects are more educative than were the semi-automatic services of slaves and menials in the older civilizations. For
the mechanical nullification of skill can take place only up to a
certain point. It is only when one has completely lost the power of
discrimination that a standardized canned soup can, without further
preparation, take the place of a home-cooked one, or when one has
lost prudence completely that a four-wheel brake can serve instead
of a good driver. Inventions like these increase the province and
multiply the interests of the amateur. When automatism becomes
general and the benefits of mechanization are socialized, men will
be back once more in the Edenlike state in which they have existed
in regions of natural increment, like the South Seas: the ritual of
leisure will replace the ritual of work, and work itself will become
a kind of game. That is, in fact, the ideal goal of a completely
mechanized and automatized system of power production: the elimination of work: the universal achievement of leisure. In his discussion of slavery Aristotle said that when the shuttle wove by itself
and the plectrum played by itself chief workmen would not need
helpers nor masters slaves. At the time he wrote, he believed that he
was establishing the eternal validity of slavery; but for us today he
was in reality justifying the existence of the machine. Work, it is
true, is the constant form of man's interaction with his environment,
if by work one means the sum total of exertions necessary to maintain life; and lack of work usually means an impairment of function
and a breakdown in organic relationship that leads to substitute forms

of work, such as invalidism and neurosis. But work in the form of unwilling drudgery or of that sedentary routine which, as Mr. Alfred Zimmern reminds us, the Athenians so properly despised—work in these degrading forms is the true province of machines. Instead of reducing human beings to work-mechanisms, we can now transfer the main part of burden to automatic machines. This potentiality, still so far from effective achievement for mankind at large, is perhaps the largest justification of the mechanical developments of the last thousand years.

From the social standpoint, one final characterization of the machine, perhaps the most important of all, must be noted: the machine imposes the necessity for collective effort and widens its range. To the extent that men have escaped the control of nature they must submit to the control of society. As in a serial operation every part must function smoothly and be geared to the right speed in order to ensure the effective working of the process as a whole, so in society at large there must be a close articulation between all its elements. Individual self-sufficiency is another way of saying technological crudeness: as our technics becomes more refined it becomes impossible to work the machine without large-scale collective cooperation, and in the long run a high technics is possible only on a basis of worldwide trade and intellectual intercourse. The machine has broken down the relative isolation—never complete even in the most primitive societies—of the handicraft period: it has intensified the need for collective effort and collective order. The efforts to achieve collective participation have been fumbling and empirical: so for the most part, people are conscious of the necessity in the form of limitations upon personal freedom and initiative—limitations like the automatic traffic signals of a congested center, or like the red-tape in a large commercial organization. The collective nature of the machine process demands a special enlargement of the imagination and a special education in order to keep the collective demand itself from becoming an act of external regimentation. To the extent that the collective discipline becomes effective and the various groups in society are worked into a nicely interlocking organization, special provisions must be made for isolated and anarchic elements that are not included in such a wide-reaching collectivism—elements that cannot without danger be ignored or repressed. But to abandon the social collectivism imposed by modern technics means to return to nature and be at the mercy of natural forces.

The regularization of time, the increase in mechanical power, the multiplication of goods, the contraction of time and space, the standardization of performance and product, the transfer of skill to automata, and the increase of collective interdependence—these, then, are the chief characteristics of our machine civilization. They are the basis of the particular forms of life and modes of expression that distinguish Western Civilization, at least in degree, from the various earlier civilizations that preceded it.

In the translation of technical improvements into social processes, however, the machine has undergone a perversion: instead of being utilized as an instrument of life, it has tended to become an absolute. Power and social control, once exercised chiefly by military groups who had conquered and seized the land, have gone since the seventeenth century to those who have organized and controlled and owned the machine. The machine has been valued because—it increased the employment of machines. And such employment was the source of profits, power, and wealth to the new ruling classes, benefits which had hitherto gone to traders or to those who monopolized the land. Jungles and tropical islands were invaded during the nineteenth century for the purpose of making new converts to the machine: explorers like Stanley endured incredible tortures and hardships in order to bring the benefits of the machine to inaccessible regions tapt by the Congo: insulated countries like Japan were entered forcibly at the point of the gun in order to make way for the trader: natives in Africa and the Americas were saddled with false debts or malicious taxes in order to give them an incentive to work and to consume in the machine fashion—and thus to supply an outlet for the goods of America and Europe, or to ensure the regular gathering of rubber and lac.

The injunction to use machines was so imperative, from the standpoint of those who owned them and whose means and place in society depended upon them, that it placed upon the worker a special burden, the duty to consume machine-products, while it placed upon the manufacturer and the engineer the duty of inventing products weak enough and shoddy enough—like the safety razor blade or the common run of American woolens—to lend themselves to rapid replacement. The great heresy to the machine was to believe in an institution or a habit of action or a system of ideas that would lessen this service to the machines: for under capitalist direction the aim of mechanism is not to save labor but to eliminate all labor except that which can be channeled at a profit through the factory.

At the beginning, the machine was an attempt to substitute quantity for value in the calculus of life. Between the conception of the machine and its utilization, as Krannhals points out, a necessary psychological and social process was skipped: the stage of evaluation. Thus a steam turbine may contribute thousands of horsepower, and a speedboat may achieve speed: but these facts, which perhaps satisfy the engineer, do not necessarily integrate them in society. Railroads may be quicker than canalboats, and a gas-lamp may be brighter than a candle: but it is only in terms of human purpose and in relation to a human and social scheme of values that speed or brightness have any meaning. If one wishes to absorb the scenery, the slow motion of a canalboat may be preferable to the fast motion of a motor car; and if one wishes to appreciate the mysterious darkness and the strange forms of a natural cave, it is better to penetrate it with uncertain steps, with the aid of a torch or a lantern, than to descend into it by means of an elevator, as in the famous caves of Virginia, and to have the mystery entirely erased by a grand display of electric lights—a commercialized perversion that puts the whole spectacle upon the low dramatic level of a cockney amusement park.

Because the process of social evaluation was largely absent among the people who developed the machine in the eighteenth and nineteenth centuries the machine raced like an engine without a governor, tending to overheat its own bearings and lower its efficiency without any compensatory gain. This left the process of evaluation to groups who remained outside the machine milieu, and who unfortunately often lacked the knowledge and the understanding that would have made their criticisms more pertinent.

The important thing to bear in mind is that the failure to evaluate
the machine and to integrate it in society as a whole was not due
simply to defects in distributing income, to errors of management, to
the greed and narrow-mindedness of the industrial leaders: it was
also due to a weakness of the entire philosophy upon which the new
techniques and inventions were grounded. The leaders and enterprisers of the period believed that they had avoided the necessity
for introducing values, except those which were automatically recorded in profits and prices. They believed that the problem of justly
distributing goods could be sidetracked by creating an abundance
of them: that the problem of applying one's energies wisely could be
cancelled out simply by multiplying them: in short, that most of the
difficulties that had hitherto vexed mankind had a mathematical or
mechanical—that is a quantitative—solution. The belief that values
could be dispensed with constituted the new system of values. Values,
divorced from the current processes of life, remained the concern of
those who reacted against the machine. Meanwhile, the current
processes justified themselves solely in terms of quantity production
and cash results. When the machine as a whole overspeeded and
purchasing power failed to keep pace with dishonest overcapitaliza-
tion and exorbitant profits—then the whole machine went suddenly
into reverse, stripped its gears, and came to a standstill: a humiliating
failure, a dire social loss.

One is confronted, then, by the fact that the machine is ambivalent.
It is both an instrument of liberation and one of repression. It has
economized human energy and it has misdirected it. It has created a
wide framework of order and it has produced muddle and chaos. It
has nobly served human purposes and it has distorted and denied
them. Before I attempt to discuss in greater detail those aspects
of the machine that have been effectively assimilated and that have
worked well, I purpose to discuss the resistances and compensations
created by the machine. For neither this new type of civilization
nor its ideal has gone unchallenged: the human spirit has not bowed
to the machine in complete submission. In every phase of existence
the machine has stirred up antipathies, dissents, reactions, some
weak, hysterical, unjustified, others that are in their nature so inevi-

table, so sound, that one cannot touch the future of the machine without taking them into account. Similarly the compensations that have arisen to overcome or mitigate the effects of the new routine of life and work call attention to dangers in the partial integration that now exists.

5: Direct Attack on the Machine

The conquest of Western Civilization by the machine was not accomplished without stubborn resistance on the part of institutions and habits and impulses which did not lend themselves to mechanical organization. From the very beginning the machine provoked compensatory or hostile reactions. In the world of ideas, romanticism and utilitarianism go side by side: Shakespeare with his cult of the individual hero and his emphasis of nationalism appeared at the same time as the pragmatic Bacon, and the emotional fervor of Wesley's Methodism spread like fire in dry grass through the very depressed classes that were subject to the new factory régime. The direct reaction of the machine was to make people materialistic and rational: its indirect action was often to make them hyper-emotional and irrational. The tendency to ignore the second set of reactions because they did not logically coincide with the claims of the machine has unfortunately been common in many critics of the new industrial order: even Veblen was not free from it.

Resistance to mechanical improvements took a wide variety of forms. The most direct and simple form was to smash the offending machine itself or to murder its inventor.

The destruction of machines and the prohibition of invention, which so beneficently transformed the society of Butler's Erewhon, might have been accomplished by the working classes of Europe but for two facts. First: the direct war against the machine was an unevenly matched struggle; for the financial and military powers were on the side of the classes that were bent on exploiting the machine, and in a pinch the soldiery, armed with their new machines, could demolish the resistance of the handworkers with a volley of musketry. As long as invention took place sporadically, the introduction of a single machine could well be retarded by direct attack: once it operated on a wide and united front no mere local rebellion could more than temporarily hold up its advance: a successful challenge would have needed a degree of organization which in the very nature of the case the working classes did not have—indeed lack even today.

The second point was equally important: life and energy and adventure were at first on the side of the machine: handicraft was associated with the fixed, the sessile, the superannuated, the dying: it manifestly shrank away from the new movements in thought and from the ordeal of the new reality. The machine meant fresh revelations, new possibilities of action: it brought with it a revolutionary élan. Youth was on its side. Seeking only the persistence of old ways, the enemies of the machine were fighting a rear-guard retreat, and they were on the side of the dead even when they espoused the organic against the mechanical.

As soon as the machine came to predominate in actual life, the only place where it could be successfully attacked or resisted was in the attitudes and interests of those who worked it. The extent to which unmechanical ideologies and programs have flourished since the seventeenth century, despite the persistent habituation of the machine, is in part a measure of the amount of resistance that the machine has, directly or indirectly, occasioned.

6: Romantic and Utilitarian

The broadest general split in ideas occasioned by the machine was that between the Romantic and the Utilitarian. Carried along by the industrial and commercial ideals of his age, the utilitarian was at one with its purposes. He believed in science and inventions, in profits and power, in machinery and progress, in money and comfort, and he believed in spreading these ideals to other societies by means of free trade, and in allowing some of the benefits to filter down from the possessing classes to the exploited—or as they are now euphemistically called, the "underprivileged"—provided that this was done prudently enough to keep the lower classes diligently at work in a state of somnolent and respectful submission.

The newness of the mechanical products was, from the utilitarian standpoint, a guarantee of their worth. The utilitarian wished to put as much distance as possible between his own society of unfettered money-making individuals and the ideals of a feudal and corporate life. These ideals, with their traditions, loyalties, sentiments, constituted a brake upon the introduction of changes and mechanical improvements: the sentiments that clustered around an old house might stand in the way of opening a mine that ran underneath it, even as the affection that often entered into the relation of master and servant under the more patriarchal older régime might stand in the way of that enlightened self-interest which would lead to the dismissal of the worker as soon as the market was slack. What most obviously prevented a clean victory of capitalistic and mechanical ideals was the tissue of ancient institutions and habits of thought: the belief that honor might be more important than money or that friendly affection and comradeship might be as powerful a motive in life as profit making: or that present animal health might be more precious than future material acquisitions—in short, that the whole man might be worth preserving at the expense of the utmost success and power of the Economic Man. Indeed, some of the sharpest criticism of the new mechanical creed came from the tory aristocrats in England, France, and in the Southern States of the United States.

Romanticism in all its manifestations, from Shakespeare to William Morris, from Goethe and the Brothers Grimm to Nietzsche, from Rousseau and Chateaubriand to Hugo, was an attempt to restore the essential activities of human life to a central place in the new scheme, instead of accepting the machine as a center, and holding all its values to be final and absolute.

In its animus, romanticism was right; for it represented those vital and historic and organic attributes that had been deliberately eliminated from the concepts of science and from the methods of the earlier technics, and it provided necessary channels of compensation. Vital organs of life, which have been amputated through historic accident, must be restored at least in fantasy, as preliminary to their actual rebuilding in fact: a psychosis is sometimes the only possible alternative to complete disruption and death. Unfortunately, in its comprehension of the forces that were at work in society the romantic movement was weak: overcome by the callous destruction that attended the introduction of the machine, it did not distinguish between the forces that were hostile to life and those that served it, but tended to lump them all in the same compartment, and to turn its back upon them. In its effort to find remedies for the dire weakness and perversions of industrial society, romanticism avoided the very energies by which alone it could hope to create a more sufficient pattern of existence—namely, the energies that were focussed in science and technics and in the mass of new machine-workers themselves. The romantic movement was retrospective, walled-in, sentimental: in a word, regressive. It lessened the shock of the new order, but it was, for the greater part, a movement of escape.

But to confess this is not to say that the romantic movement was unimportant or unjustified. On the contrary, one cannot comprehend the typical dilemmas of the new civilization unless one understands the reason and the rationale of the romantic reaction against it, and sees how necessary it is to import the positive elements in the romantic attitude into the new social synthesis. Romanticism as an *alternative* to the machine is dead: indeed it never was alive: but the forces and ideas once archaically represented by romanticism are necessary ingredients in the new civilization, and the need today is to translate them into direct social modes of expression, instead of continuing them in the old form of an unconscious or deliberate regression into a past that can be retrieved only in phantasy.

The romantic reaction took many forms: and I shall consider only the three dominant ones: the cult of history and nationalism, the cult of nature, and the cult of the primitive. The same period saw likewise the cult of the isolated individual, and the revival of old theologies and theosophies and supernaturalisms, which owed their existence and much of their strength no doubt to the same denials and emptinesses that prompted the more specially romantic revivals: but it is next to impossible to distinguish clearly between the continued interests of religion and their modern revivals; so I shall confine this analysis to the romantic reaction proper; for this plainly accompanied and probably grew out of the new situation.

7: The Cult of the Past

The cult of the past did not immediately develop in response to the machine; it was, in Italy, an attempt to resume the ideas and forms of classic civilization, and during the Renascence the cult was, in fact, a sort of secret ally to the machine. Did it not, like the machine, challenge the validity of the existing traditions in both philosophy and daily life? Did it not give more authority to the manuscripts of ancient authors, to Hero of Alexandria in physics, to Vitruvius in architecture, to Columella in farming, than it did to the existing body of tradition and the practices of contemporary masters? Did it not, by breaking with the immediate past, encourage the future to break with the present?

The recovery of the classic past during the Renascence caused a break in the historic continuity of Western Europe; and this gap, which opened in education and the formal arts, made a breach of which the machine promptly took advantage. By the eighteenth century the Renascence culture itself was sterilized, pedanticized, formalized: it gave itself over to the recovery and reproduction of dead forms; and though a Poussin or a Piranesi could revitalize these forms with a little of the flair and confidence that the men of the late fifteenth century had felt, the neo-classic and the mechanical played into each other's hands: in the sense of being divorced from life, the first was even more mechanical than mechanism itself. It is not perhaps altogether an accident that at a distance the palaces of Versailles and St. Petersburg have the aspect of modern factory buildings. When the cult of the past revived again, it was directed against both the arid humanism of the eighteenth century and the equally arid dehumanism of the mechanical age. William Blake, with his usual true instinct for fundamental differences, attacked with equal vehemence Sir Joshua Reynolds and Sir Isaac Newton.

In the eighteenth century a cultured man was one who knew his Greek and Latin classics; an enlightened man was one who regarded any part of the globe as suitable for human habitation, provided that its laws were just and their administration impartial; a man of taste was one who knew that standards of proportion and beauty in architecture and sculpture and painting had been fixed forever by classic precedent. The living tissue of customs and traditions, the vernacular architecture, the folkways and the folk-tales, the vulgar languages and dialects that were spoken outside Paris and London— all these things were looked upon by the eighteenth century gentleman as a mass of follies and barbarisms. Enlightenment and progress meant the spreading of London, Paris, Vienna, Berlin, Madrid, and St. Petersburg over wider and wider areas.

Thanks to the dominance of the machine, to books and bayonets, to printed calicos and missionary pocket-handkerchiefs, to brumma-gem jewelry and cutlery and beads, a layer of this civilization began to spread like a film of oil over the planet at large: machine tex-tiles supplanted hand-woven ones, aniline dyes eventually took the place of vegetable dyes locally made, and even in distant Polynesia calico dresses and stove-pipe hats and shame covered up the proud bodies of the natives, while syphilis and rum, introduced at the same time as the Bible, added a special physical horror to their degrada-tion. Wherever this film of oil spread, the living fish were poisoned and their bloated bodies rose to the surface of the water, adding their own decay to the stench of the oil itself. The new mechanical civilization respected neither place nor past. In the reaction that it provoked place and past were the two aspects of existence that were over-stressed.

This reaction appeared definitely in the eighteenth century, just at the moment that the paleotechnic revolution was getting under way. It began as an attempt to take up the old threads of life at the point where the Renascence had dropped them: it was thus a return to the Middle Ages and a re-reading of their significance, absurdly by Walpole, coldly by Robert Adam, graphically by Scott, faithfully by von Scheffel, esthetically by Goethe and Blake, piously by Pugin and the members of the Oxford movement, moralistically by Carlyle and Ruskin, imaginatively by Victor Hugo. These poets and architects and critics disclosed once more the wealth and interest of the old local life in Europe: they showed how much engineering had lost by deserting gothic forms for the simpler post and lintel construction of classic architecture, and how much literature had forfeited by its extravagant interest in classic forms and themes and its snobbish parade of classic allusions, while the most poignant emotions were embodied in the local ballads that still lingered on in the countryside.

By this "gothic" revival a slight check was placed upon the centralizing, exploitative, and de-regionalizing processes of the machine civilization. Local folk lore and local fairy tales were collected by scholars like the Brothers Grimm and historically minded novelists like Scott; local monuments of archaeology were preserved, and the glorious stained glass and wall paintings of the medieval and early Renascence churches were saved here and there from the glazier and plasterer, still erasing these remnants of "gothic barbarity" in the name of progress and good taste. Local legends were collected: indeed, one of the most remarkable poems of the romantic movement, Tam O'Shanter, was written merely to serve as letterpress for a picture of Alloway's auld haunted kirk. Most potent of all, local languages and dialects were pounced upon, in the very act of dying, and restored to life by turning them to literary uses.

The nationalist movement took advantage of these new cultural interests and attempted to use them for the purpose of fortifying the political power of the unified nationalist state, that mighty engine for preserving the economic *status quo* and for carrying out imperialistic policies of aggression among the weaker races. In this manner, amorphous entities like Germany and Italy became self-conscious and realized a certain degree of political self-sufficiency. But the new interests and revivals struck much deeper than political nationalism, and were more concentrated in their sphere of action: moreover, they touched aspects of life to which a mere power politics was as indifferent as was a power economics. The creation of nationalist states was essentially a movement of protest against alien political powers, wielded without the consent and participation of the governed: a protest against the largely arbitrary political groupings of the dynastic period. But the nations, once they achieved independent nationality, speedily began with the introduction of coal-industrialism to go through the same process of de-regionalization as those that had had no separate national existence; and it was only with the growth of a more intensive and self-conscious regionalism that the process began to work in the opposite direction.

The revival of place interests and language interests, focussed in the new appreciation of regional history, is one of the definite characteristics of nineteenth century culture. Because it was in direct conflict with the cosmopolitan free-trade imperialism of the leading economic thought of the period—and political economy had a hallowed status among the social sciences during this period, because of its useful mythological character—this new regionalism was never carefully appraised or sufficiently appreciated in the early days of its existence. Even now it is still often looked upon as a queer aberration: for plainly it does not fit in altogether with the doctrines of industrial world-conquest or with those of "progress." The movement did not in fact crystallize, despite the valuable preliminary work of the romantics, until the middle of the nineteenth century; and instead of disappearing with the more universal triumph of the machine it went on after that with accelerating speed and intensity. First France: then Denmark: now every part of the world has felt at least a tremor of the countering shock of regionalism, sometimes a definite upheaval.

At the beginning, the main impulse came from the historic regions whose existence was threatened by the mechanical and political unifications of the nineteenth century. The movement had indeed a definite beginning in time, namely 1854; in that year occurred the first meeting of the Félibrigistes, who gathered together for the purpose of restoring the language and the autonomous cultural life of Provence. The Provençal language had all but been destroyed by the Albigensian crusades: Provence had been, so to say, a conquered province of the Church, which had decimated it by a strenuous use of the secular arm; and although an attempt had been made by the Seven Poets of Toulouse, in 1324, to revive the language, the movement had not succeeded: the speech of Ronsard and Racine had finally prevailed. In their consciousness of the part played by language as a means of establishing and helping to build up their identity with their region, a group of literary men, headed by Frédéric Mistral, started to institute the regionalist movement.

This movement has gone through a similar set of stages in every country where it has taken place: in Denmark, in Norway, in Ireland, in Catalonia, in Brittany, in Wales, in Scotland, in Palestine, and similar signs are already visible in various regions in North America. There is, as M. Jourdanne has put it, at first a poetic cycle: this leads to the recovery of the language and literature of the folk, and the attempt to use it as a vehicle for contemporary expression on the basis of largely traditional forms. The second is the cycle of prose, in which the interest in the language leads to an interest in the totality of a community's life and history, and so brings the movement directly onto the contemporary stage. And finally there is the cycle of action, in which regionalism forms for itself fresh objectives, political, economic, civic, cultural, on the basis, not of a servile restoration of the past, but of a growing integration of the new forces that have attached themselves to the main trunk of tradition. The only places where regionalism has not been militantly self-conscious are places like the cities and provinces of Germany in which—until the recent centralization of power by the Totalitarian State—an autonomous and effective local life had never entirely disappeared.

The besetting weakness of regionalism lies in the fact that it is in part a blind reaction against outward circumstances and disruptions, an attempt to find refuge within an old shell against the turbulent invasions of the outside world, armed with its new engines: in short, an aversion from what is, rather than an impulse toward what may be. For the merely sentimental regionalist, the past was an absolute. His impulse was to fix some definite moment in the past, and to keep on living it over and over again, holding the "original" regional costumes, which were in fact merely the fashion of a certain century, maintaining the regional forms of architecture, which were merely the most convenient and comely constructions at a certain moment of cultural and technical development; and he sought, more or less, to keep these "original" customs and habits and interests fixed forever in the same mould: a neurotic retreat. In that sense regionalism, it seems plain, was anti-historical and anti-organic: for it denied both the fact of change and the possibility that anything of value could come out of it.

While it would be dishonest to gloss over this weakness, one must understand it in terms of the circumstances that conspired to produce it. It was a flat reaction against the equally exaggerated neglect of the traditions and historic monuments of a community's life, fostered by the abstractly progressive minds of the nineteenth century. For the new industrialist, "history was bunk." Is it any wonder that the new regionalist overcompensated for that contempt and ignorance by holding that even the dustiest relics of the past were sacred? What was mistaken was not the interest but the tactics. Vis-a-vis the machine, the regionalist was in the position of a swimmer facing a strong incoming tide: if he attempts to stand up against the high waves he is knocked down: if he seeks safety by retreating unaided to the shore, he is caught in the undertow of the receding wave and can neither reach land nor keep his footing: his welfare depends upon his confidence in meeting the wave and plunging along with it at the moment it is about to break, thus utilizing the energy of the very force he is attempting to escape. These were the tactics of Bishop Grundtvig of Denmark, who not merely revived the old ballads but founded the cooperative agricultural movement: they are the basis of a dynamic regionalism.

The fact is, at all events, that the development of local languages and regional cultures, though springing immediately perhaps out of a reactionary impulse, was not limited to negations, neither was it hopelessly remote from those currents of modern life which strengthen the bonds between regions and universalize the common benefits of Western Civilization: it was rather complementary to them. A world that is united physically by the airplane, the radio, the cable, must eventually, if cooperation is to increase, devise a common language to take care of all its practical matters—its news despatches, its business communications, its international broadcasts, and the relatively simple needs and curiosities of travellers. Precisely as the boundaries of mechanical intercourse widen and become worldwide, a universal language must supplant the tongue of even the most influential national aggregation. From this point of view, one of the worst blows to internationalism was that struck by the pedants of the Renascence when in their worship of the classics they abandoned scholastic Latin, the universal language of the learned classes.

But along with this pragmatic development of a common tongue a more intimate language is needed for the deeper sort of cooperation and communication. Languages equipped for this special cultural purpose have been spontaneously growing up or reviving all over the Western World from the middle of the nineteenth century onwards. Welsh, Gaelic, Hebrew, Catalan, Flemish, Czech, Norwegian, Landsmåal, Africaans are some of the languages that are either new, or have been renovated and popularized recently for combined vernacular and literary use. While the growth of travel and communication will doubtless lead to a consolidation of dialects, reducing, say, the three hundred odd languages of India to a handful of major languages, it is already being counteracted by the opposite process of re-differentiation: the gap between English and American is much wider now than it was when Noah Webster codified the slightly more archaic American forms and pronunciations.

There is no reason to think that any single national language can now dominate the world, as the French and the English people have by turns dreamed: for unless an international language can be made relatively fixed and lifeless, it will go through a babel-like differentiation in precisely the same fashion as Latin did. It is much more likely that bi-lingualism will become universal—that is, an arranged and purely artificial world-language for pragmatic and scientific uses, and a cultural language for local communication.

The revival of these cultural languages and literatures and the stimulation of local life that has resulted from their use, must be counted as one of the most effective measures society has taken for protection against the automatic processes of machine civilization. Against the dream of universal and complete standardization, the dream of the universal cockney, and of one long street, called the Tottenham Court Road or Broadway threading over the globe, and of one language spoken everywhere and on all occasions—against this now archaic dream one must place the fact of cultural re-individuation. While the reaction has often been blind and ̄arbitrary, it has been no more so than the equally "forward-looking" movements it was attempting to halt. Behind it lies the human need to control the machine, if not at the point of origin, then at the point of application.

8: The Return to Nature

The historical revival of regionalism was re-enforced by another movement: the Return to Nature.

The cultivation of nature for its own sake, and the pursuit of rural modes of living and the appreciation of the rural environment became in the eighteenth century one of the chief means of escaping the counting house and the machine. So long as the country was uppermost, the cult of nature could have no meaning: being a part of life, there was no need to make it a special object of thought. It was only when the townsman found himself closed in by his methodical urban routine and deprived in his new urban environment of the sight of sky and grass and trees, that the value of the country manifested itself clearly to him. Before this, an occasional rare adventurer would seek the solitude of the mountains to cultivate his soul: but in the eighteenth century Jean-Jacques Rousseau, preaching the wisdom of the peasant and the sanity of the simple rural occupations, led a whole succession of generations outside the gates of their cities: they botanized, they climbed mountains, they sang peasant songs, they swam in the moonlight, they helped in the harvest field; and those who could afford to built .themselves rural retreats. This impulse to recapture nature had a powerful influence upon the cultivation of the environment as a whole and upon the development of cities: but I reserve this for discussion in another book.

The important thing is to realize that at the very moment life was becoming more constricted and routinized, a great safety valve for the aboriginal human impulses had been found—the raw, unexplored, and relatively uncultivated regions of America and Africa, and even the less formidable islands of the South Seas: above all, the most steadfast of primitive environments, the ocean, had been thrown open to the discontented and the adventurous. Failing to accept the destiny that the inventors and the industrialists were creating, failing to welcome the comforts and the conveniences of civilized existence and accept the high value placed upon them by the reigning bourgeoisie, those who possessed hardier virtues and a quicker sense of values could escape from the machine. In the forests and grasslands of the new worlds they could wring a living from the soil, and on the sea they could face the elemental forces of wind and water. Here, likewise, those too weak to face the machine could find temporary refuge.

This solution was perhaps almost a too perfect one: for the new settlers and pioneers not merely satisfied their own spiritual needs by colonizing the less inhabited areas of the globe, but in the act of so doing they provided raw materials for the new industries, they likewise afforded a market for their manufactured goods, and they paved the way for the eventual introduction of the machine. Rarely have the inner impulses of different parts of society balanced so neatly with the outer conditions of its success: rarely has there been a social situation which was satisfactory to so many different types of personality and so many varieties of human effort. For a brief hundred years—roughly from 1790 to 1890 in North America, and perhaps a little earlier and a little later for South America and Africa—the land pioneer and the industrial pioneer were in close partnership. The thrifty, aggressive, routinized men built their factories and regimented their workers: the tough, sanguine, spirited, non-mechanical men fought the aborigines, cleared the land, scoured the forests for game and clove the virgin soils with their plows. If the new agricultural opportunities were still too tame and respectable, even though old customs and solidarities were disregarded and old precedents flouted, there were horses to be roped on the pampas, petroleum to be tapt in Pennsylvania, gold was to be found in California and Australia, rubber and tea to be planted in the East, and virgin lands in the steaming heart of Africa or in the coldest north could be trodden for the first time by white men, seeking food or knowledge or adventure or psychal remoteness from their own kind.

Not until the new lands were completely occupied and exploited did the machine come in, to claim its special form of dominion over those who had shown neither courage nor luck nor cunning in exploiting Nature. For millions of men and women, the new lands staved off the moment of submission. By accepting the shackles of nature they could evade for a brief while the complicated interdependence of the machine civilization. The more humane or fanatic types, in the company of their fellows, could even make an equally brief effort to realize their dream of the perfect society or the Heavenly City: from the Shaker colonies in New England to the Mormons of Utah there stretched a weak faint line of perfectionists, seeking to circumvent both the aimless brutality of nature and the more purposeful brutality of man.

Movements as vast and complex as the migration of peoples from the seventeenth to the twentieth century cannot of course be accounted for by a single cause or a single set of circumstances. The pressure of population-growth by itself is not sufficient to explain it, for not merely did the movement precede the growth, but the fact is that this pressure was considerably eased in Europe by the introduction of the potato, the improvement of the winter cattle fodder crops and the overthrow of the three-field system, at the very moment that the exodus to the new world was greatly accelerated. Nor can it be explained on purely political terms as an attempt to escape obsolete ecclesiastical and political institutions, or a result of the desire to breathe the free unpolluted air of republican institutions. Nor again was it merely a practical working out of the desire to return to Nature, although Rousseau had plainly influenced people who talked Rousseau and acted Rousseau without ever perhaps having heard his name. But all these motives were in existence: the desire to be free from social compulsion, the desire for economic security, the desire to return to nature; and they played into each other's hands. They provided both the excuse and the motive power for escaping from the new mechanical civilization that was closing in upon the Western World. To shoot, to trap, to chop trees, to hold a plow, to prospect, to face a seam—all these primitive occupations, out of which technics had originally sprung, all these occupations that had been closed and stabilized by the very advances of technics, were now open to the pioneer: he might be hunter, fisher, miner, woodman, and farmer by turn, and by engaging in these occupations people could restore their plain animal vigor as men and women, temporarily freed from the duties of a more orderly and servile existence.

Within a short century this savage idyll practically came to an end. The industrial pioneer caught up with the land pioneer and the latter could only rehearse in play what his forefathers had done out of sheer necessity. But as long as the opportunities were open in the unsettled countries, people took advantage of them in numbers that would be astounding if the blessings of an orderly, acquisitive, mechanized civilization were as great as the advocates of Progress believed and preached. Millions of people chose a lifetime of danger, heroic toil, deprivation and hardships, battling with the forces of Nature, rather than accept life on the terms that it was offered alike to the victorious and the vanquished in the new hives of industry. The movement was in part the reverse of that great organizing effort of the eleventh and twelfth centuries which cleared the forests and marshes and erected cities from one end of Europe to the other: it was rather a tendency to disperse, to escape from a close, systematic, cultivated life into an open and relatively barbarous existence.

With the occupation of the remaining open lands, this modern movement of population tapered off, and our mechanical civilization lost one of its main safety valves. The most simple human reaction that fear of the machine could provoke—running away from it—had ceased to be possible without undermining the basis of livelihood. So complete has the victory of the machine been during the last generation that in the periodic exodus from the machine which takes place on holidays in America the would-be exiles escape in motor cars and carry into the wilderness a phonograph or a radio set. And ultimately, then, the reaction of the pioneer was far less effective, though it so soon found practical channels, than the romanticism of the poets and architects and painters who merely created in the mind the ideal image of a more humane life.

Yet the lure of more primitive conditions of life, as an alternative to the machine, remains. Some of those who shrink from the degree of social control necessary to operate the machine rationally, are now busy with plans for scrapping the machine and returning to a bare subsistence level in little island utopias devoted to sub-agriculture

and sub-manufacture. The advocates of these measures for returning
to the primitive forget only one fact: what they are proposing is not
an adventure but a bedraggled retreat, not a release but a confession
of complete failure. They propose to return to the physical conditions
of pioneer existence without the positive spiritual impulse that made
the original conditions tolerable and the original efforts possible. If
such defeatism becomes widespread it would mean something more
than the collapse of the machine: it would mean the end of the present
cycle of Western Civilization.

9: Organic and Mechanical Polarities

During the century and a half that followed Rousseau the cult of
the primitive took many forms. Joining up with historical romanticism, which had other roots, it expressed itself on the imaginative
level as an interest in the folk arts and in the products of primitive
people, no longer dismissed as crude and barbarous, but valued
precisely for these qualities, which were often conspicuously lacking
in more highly developed communities. Not by accident was the interest in the art of the African negroes, one of the manifestations of
this cult in our century, the product of the same group of Parisian
painters who accepted with utmost heartiness the new forms of the
machine: Congo maintained the balance against the motor works
and the subway.

But on the wider platform of personal behavior, the primitive
disclosed itself during the twentieth century in the insurgence of sex.
The erotic dances of the Polynesians, the erotic music of the African
negro tribes, these captured the imagination and presided over the
recreation of the mechanically disciplined urban masses of Western
Civilization, reaching their swiftest development in the United States,
the country that had most insistently fostered mechanical gadgets
and mechanical routines. To the once dominantly masculine relaxation of drunkenness was added the hetero-sexual relaxation of the
dance and the erotic embrace, two phases of the sexual act that were
now performed in public. The reaction grew in proportion to the external restraint imposed by the day's grind; but instead of enriching
the erotic life and providing deep organic satisfactions, these com-

pensatory measures tended to keep sex at a constant pitch of stimulation and ultimately of irritation: for the ritual of sexual excitation
pervaded not merely recreation but business: it appeared in the office
and the advertisement, to remind and to tantalize without providing
sufficient occasions for active release.

The distinction between sexual expression as one of the modes of
life and sex as a compensating element in a monotonous and restricted existence must not be lost, even though it be difficult to define.
For sex, I need hardly say, manifested itself in both forms during
this period, and with the positive side of this development and its
many fruitful and far-reaching consequences, I purpose to deal at
length in another place. But in its extreme forms, the compensatory
element could easily be detected: for it was marked by an abstract-
ness and a remoteness, derived from the very environment that the
populace was desperately trying to escape. The weakness of these
primitive compensations disclosed itself in the usually synthetic
obscenities of the popular joke, the remote glamor of the embraces
of moving picture stars, the voluptuous contortions of dancers on the
stage and of experiences taken in at second or third hand through the
bawdy mimicry of the popular song or, a little closer to reality,
snatched hastily and furtively at the end of an automobile ride or a
fatiguing day in the office or the factory. Those who escaped the
anxiety and frustration of such embraces did so only by deadening
their higher nerve-centers by means of alcohol or by the chemistry
of some form of psychal anesthesia which took the outward form of
coarseness and debasement.

In brief, most of the sexual compensations were little above the
level of abject fantasy; whereas when sex is accepted as an important
mode of life, lovers reject these weak and secondary substitutes for
it, and devote their minds and energies to courtship and expression
themselves: necessary steps to those enlargements and enrichments
and sublimations of sex that alike maintain the species and energize
the entire cultural heritage. It was a miner's son, D. H. Lawrence,
who distinguished most sharply between the degradation of sex which
occurs when it is merely a means of getting away from the sordid
environment and oppressive dullness of a low-grade industrial town,

and the exhilaration that arises when sex is genuinely respected and celebrated in its own right.

The weakness of the sexual relapse into the primitive was not indeed unlike that which overtook the more general cultivation of the body through sport. The impulse that excited it was genuine and justified; but the form it took did not lead to a transformation of the original condition: rather, it became the mechanism by means of which the original condition was remedied sufficiently to continue in existence. Sex had a larger part of life to claim than it filched for itself in the instinctive reaction against the machine.

As the machine tended toward the pole of regularity and complete automatism, it became severed, finally, from the umbilical cord that bound it to the bodies of men and women: it became an absolute. That was the danger Samuel Butler jestingly prophesied in Erewhon, the danger that the human being might become a means whereby the machine perpetuated itself and extended its dominion. The recoil from the absolute of mechanism was into an equally sterile absolute of the organic: the raw primitive. The organic processes, reduced to shadows by the machine, made a violent effort to retrieve their position. The machine, which acerbically denied the flesh, was offset by the flesh, which denied the rational, the intelligent, the orderly processes of behavior that have entered into all man's cultural developments—even those developments that most closely derive from the organic. The spurious notion that mechanism had naught to learn from life was supplanted by the equally false notion that life had nothing to learn from mechanism. On one side is the gigantic printing press, a miracle of fine articulation, which turns out the tabloid newspaper: on the other side are the contents of the tabloid itself, symbolically recording the most crude and elementary states of emotion, feeling, barely vestigial thought. Here the impersonal and the cooperative and the objective: over against it the limited, the subjective, the recalcitrant, violent ego, full of hatreds, fears, blind frenzies, crude impulses toward destruction. Mechanical instruments, potentially a vehicle of rational human purposes, are scarcely a blessing when they enable the gossip of the village idiot and the deeds of the thug to be broadcast to a million people each day.

The effect of this return to the absolute primitive, like so many other neurotic adaptations that temporarily bridge the chasm, develops stresses of its own which tend to push the two sides of existence still further apart. That hiatus limits the efficiency of the compensatory reaction: ultimately it spells ruin for the civilization that seeks to maintain the raw mechanical by weighting it with the raw primitive. For in its broadest reaches, including all those cultural interests and sentiments and admirations which sustain the work of the scientist, the technician, the artist, the philosopher, even when they do not appear directly in the particular work itself—in its broadest reaches this civilization cannot be run by barbarians. A hairy ape in the stokehold is a grave danger signal: a hairy ape on the bridge means speedy shipwreck. The appearance of such apes, in the forms of those political dictators who attempt to accomplish by calculated brutality and aggression what they lack the intelligence and magnanimity to consummate by more humane direction, indicates on what an infirm and treacherous foundation the machine at present rests. For, more disastrous than any mere physical destruction of machines by the barbarian is his threat to turn off or divert the human motive power, discouraging the cooperative processes of thought and the disinterested research which are responsible for our major technical achievements.

Toward the end of his life Herbert Spencer viewed with proper alarm the regression into imperialism, militarism, servility that he saw all around him at the beginning of the present century; and in truth he had every reason for his forebodings. But the point is that these forces were not merely archaic survivals that had failed to be extirpated by the machine: they were rather underlying human elements awakened into stertorous activity by the very victory of the machine as an absolute and non-conditioned force in human life. The machine, by failing as yet—despite neotechnic advances—to allow sufficient play in social existence to the organic, has opened the way for its return in the narrow and inimical form of the primitive. Western society is relapsing at critical points into pre-civilized modes of thought, feeling, and action because it has acquiesced too easily in the dehumanization of society through capitalist exploitation and military conquest. The retreat into the primitive is, in sum, a maudlin effort to avoid the more basic and infinitely more difficult transformation which our thinkers and leaders and doers have lacked the candor to face, the intelligence to contrive, and the will to effect—the transition beyond the historic forms of capitalism and the equally limited original forms of the machine to a life-centered economy.

10: Sport and the "Bitch-goddess"

The romantic movements were important as a corrective to the machine because they called attention to essential elements in life that were left out of the mechanical world-picture: they themselves prepared some of the materials for a richer synthesis. But there is within modern civilization a whole series of compensatory functions that, so far from making better integration possible, only serve to stabilize the existing state—and finally they themselves become part of the very regimentation they exist to combat. The chief of these institutions is perhaps mass-sports. One may define these sports as those forms of organized play in which the spectator is more important than the player, and in which a good part of the meaning is lost when the game is played for itself. Mass-sport is primarily a spectacle.

Unlike play, mass-sport usually requires an element of mortal chance or hazard as one of its main ingredients: but instead of the chance's occurring spontaneously, as in mountain climbing, it must take place in accordance with the rules of the game and must be increased when the spectacle begins to bore the spectators. Play in one form or another is found in every human society and among a great many animal species: but sport in the sense of a mass-spectacle, with death to add to the underlying excitement, comes into existence when a population has been drilled and regimented and depressed to such an extent that it needs at least a vicarious participation in difficult feats of strength or skill or heroism in order to sustain its waning life-sense. The demand for circuses, and when the milder spectacles are still insufficiently life-arousing, the demand for sadistic exploits and finally for blood is characteristic of civilizations that are losing their grip: Rome under the Caesars, Mexico at the time of Montezuma, Germany under the Nazis. These forms of surrogate manliness and bravado are the surest signs of a collective impotence and a pervasive death wish. The dangerous symptoms of that ultimate decay one finds everywhere today in machine civilization under the guise of mass-sport.

The invention of new forms of sport and the conversion of play into sport were two of the distinctive marks of the last century: baseball is an example of the first, and the transformation of tennis and golf into tournament spectacles, within our own day, is an example of the second. Unlike play, sport has an existence in our mechanical civilization even in its most abstract possible manifestation: the crowd that does not witness the ball game will huddle around the scoreboard in the metropolis to watch the change of counters. If it does not see the aviator finish a record flight around the world, it will listen over the radio to the report of his landing and hear the frantic shouts of the mob on the field: should the hero attempt to avoid a public reception and parade, he would be regarded as cheating. At times, as in horse-racing, the elements may be reduced to names and betting odds: participation need go no further than the newspaper and the betting booth, provided that the element of chance be there. Since the principal aim of our mechanical routine in industry is to reduce the domain of chance, it is in the glorification of chance and the unexpected, which sport provides, that the element extruded by the machine returns, with an accumulated emotional charge, to life in general. In the latest forms of mass-sport, like air races and motor races, the thrill of the spectacle is intensified by the promise of immediate death or fatal injury. The cry of horror that escapes from the crowd when the motor car overturns or the airplane crashes is not one of surprise but of fulfilled expectation: is it not fundamentally for the sake of exciting just such bloodlust that the competition itself is held and widely attended? By means of the talking picture that spectacle and that thrill are repeated in a thousand theatres throughout the world as a mere incident in the presentation of the week's news: so that a steady habituation to blood-letting and exhibitionistic murder and suicide accompanies the spread of the machine and, becoming stale by repetition in its milder forms, encourages the demand for more massive and desperate exhibitions of brutality.

Sport presents three main elements: the spectacle, the competition, and the personalities of the gladiators. The spectacle itself introduces the esthetic element, so often lacking in the paleotechnic industrial environment itself. The race is run or the game is played within a frame of spectators, tightly massed: the movements of this mass, their cries, their songs, their cheers, are a constant accompaniment of the spectacle: they play, in effect, the part of the Greek chorus in the new machine-drama, announcing what is about to occur and under-lining the events of the contest. Through his place in the chorus, the spectator finds his special release: usually cut off from close physical associations by his impersonal routine, he is now at one with a primi-tive undifferentiated group. His muscles contract or relax with the progress of the game, his breath comes quick or slow, his shouts heighten the excitement of the moment and increase his internal sense of the drama: in moments of frenzy he pounds his neighbor's back or embraces him. The spectator feels himself contributing by his pres-ence to the victory of his side, and sometimes, more by hostility to the enemy than encouragement to the friend, he does perhaps exercize a visible effect on the contest. It is a relief from the passive rôle of taking orders and automatically filling them, of conforming by means of a reduced "I" to a magnified "It," for in the sports arena the spectator has the illusion of being completely mobilized and utilized. Moreover, the spectacle itself is one of the richest satis-factions for the esthetic sense that the machine civilization offers to those that have no key to any other form of culture: the spectator knows the style of his favorite contestants in the way that the painter knows the characteristic line or palette of his master, and he reacts to the bowler, the pitcher, the punter, the server, the air ace, with a view, not only to his success in scoring, but to the esthetic spectacle itself. This point has been stressed in bull-fighting; but of course it applies to every form of sport. There remains, nevertheless, a conflict between the desire for a skilled exhibition and the desire for a brutal outcome: the maceration or death of one or more of the contestants.

Now in the competition two elements are in conflict: chance and record-making. Chance is the sauce that stimulates the excitement of the spectator and increases his zest for gambling: whippet-racing and horse-racing are as effective in this relation as games where a greater degree of human skill is involved. But the habits of the mechanical régime are as difficult to combat in sport as in the realm of sexual behavior: hence one of the most significant elements in modern sport is the fact that an abstract interest in record-making has become one of its main preoccupations. To cut.the fifth of a second off the time of running a race, to swim the English channel twenty minutes faster than another swimmer, to stay up in the air an hour longer than one's rival did—these interests come into the competition and turn it from a purely human contest to one in which the real opponent is the previous record: time takes the place of a visible rival. Sometimes, as in dance marathons or flag-pole squattings, the record goes to feats of inane endurance: the blankest and dreariest of sub-human spectacles. With the increase in professionalized skill that accompanies this change, the element of chance is further reduced: the sport, which was originally a drama, becomes an exhibition. As soon as specialism reaches this point, the whole performance is arranged as far as possible for the end of making possible the victory of the popular favorite: the other contestants are, so to say, thrown to the lions. Instead of "Fair Play" the rule now becomes "Success at Any Price."

Finally, in addition to the spectacle and the competition, there comes onto the stage, further to differentiate sport from play, the new type of popular hero, the professional player or sportsman. He is as specialized for the vocation as a soldier or an opera singer: he represents virility, courage, gameness, those talents in exercizing and commanding the body which have so small a part in the new mechanical regimen itself: if the hero is a girl, her qualities must be Amazonian in character. The sports hero represents the masculine virtues, the Mars complex, as the popular motion picture actress or the bathing beauty contestant represents Venus. He exhibits that complete skill to which the amateur vainly aspires. Instead of being looked upon as a servile and ignoble being, because of the very perfection of his physical efforts, as the Athenians in Socrates' time looked upon the professional athletes and dancers, this new hero represents the summit of the amateur's effort, not at pleasure but at efficiency. The hero is handsomely paid for his efforts, as well as being rewarded by praise and publicity, and he thus further restores to sport its connection with the very commercialized existence from which it is supposed to provide relief—restores it and thereby sanctifies it. Tne few heroes who resist this vulgarization—notably Lindbergh—fall into popular or at least into journalistic disfavor, for they are only playing the less important part of the game. The really successful sports hero, to satisfy the mass-demand, must be midway between a pander and a prostitute.

Sport, then, in this mechanized society, is no longer a mere game empty of any reward other than the playing: it is a profitable business: millions are invested in arenas, equipment, and players, and the maintenance of sport becomes as important as the maintenance of any other form of profit-making mechanism. And the technique of mass-sport infects other activities: scientific expeditions and geographic explorations are conducted in the manner of a speed stunt or a prizefight—*and for the same reason.* Business or recreation or mass spectacle, sport is always a means: even when it is reduced to athletic and military exercizes held with great pomp within the sports arenas, the aim is to gather a record-breaking crowd of performers and spectators, and thus testify to the success or importance of the movement that is represented. Thus sport, which began originally, perhaps, as a spontaneous reaction against the machine, has become one of the mass-duties of the machine age. It is a part of that universal regimentation of life—for the sake of private profits or nationalistic exploit—from which its excitement provides a temporary and only a superficial release. Sport has turned out, in short, to be one of the least effective reactions against the machine. There is only one other reaction less effective in its final result: the most ambitious as well as the most disastrous. I mean war.

11: The Cult of Death

Conflict, of which war is a specialized institutional drama, is a recurrent fact in human societies: it is indeed inevitable when society has reached any degree of differentiation, because the absence of conflict would presume a unanimity that exists only in placentals between embryos and their female parents. The desire to achieve that kind of unity is one of the most patently regressive characteristics of totalitarian states and other similar attempts at tyranny in smaller groups.

But war is that special form of conflict in which the aim is not to resolve the points of difference but to annihilate physically the defenders of opposing points or reduce them by force to submission. And whereas conflict is an inevitable incident in any active system of cooperation, to be welcomed just because of the salutary variations and modifications it introduces, war is plainly a specialized perversion of conflict, bequeathed perhaps by the more predatory hunting groups; and it is no more an eternal and necessary phenomenon in group life than is cannibalism or infanticide.

War differs in scale, in intention, in deadliness, and in frequency with the type of society: it ranges all the way from the predominantly ritualistic warfare of many primitive societies to the ferocious slaughters instituted from time to time by barbarian conquerors like Ghengis Khan and the systematic combats between entire nations that now occupy so much of the time and energy and attention of "advanced" and "peaceful" industrial countries. The impulses toward destruction have plainly not decreased with progress in the means: indeed there is some reason to think that our original collecting and food-gathering ancestors, before they had invented weapons to aid them in hunting, were more peaceful in habit than their more civilized descendants. As war has increased in destructiveness, the sporting element has grown smaller. Legend tells of an ancient conqueror who spurned to capture a town by surprise at night because it would be too easy and would take away the glory: today a well-organized army attempts to exterminate the enemy by artillery fire before it advances to capture the position.

In almost all its manifestations, however, war indicates a throwback to an infantile psychal pattern on the part of people who can no longer stand the exacting strain of life in groups, with all the necessities for compromise, give-and-take, live-and-let-live, understanding and sympathy that such life demands, and with all the complexities of adjustment involved. They seek by the knife and the gun to unravel the social knot. But whereas national wars today are essentially collective competitions in which the battlefield takes the place of the market, the ability of war to command the loyalty and interests of the entire underlying population rests partly upon its peculiar psychological reactions: it provides an outlet and an emotional release. "Art degraded, imagination denied," as Blake says, "war governed the nations."

For war is the supreme drama of a completely mechanized society; and it has an element of advantage that puts it high above all the other preparatory forms of mass-sport in which the attitudes of war are mimicked: war is real, while in all the other mass-sports there is an element of make-believe: apart from the excitements of the game and the gains or losses from gambling, it does not really matter who is victorious. In war, there is no doubt as to the reality: success may bring the reward of death just as surely as failure, and it may bring it to the remotest spectator as well as to the gladiators in the center of the vast arena of the nations.

But war, for those actually engaged in combat, likewise brings a release from the sordid motives of profit-making and self-seeking that govern the prevailing forms of business enterprise, including sport: the action has the significance of high drama. And while warfare is one of the principal sources of mechanism, and its drill and regimentation are the very pattern of old-style industrial effort, it provides, far more than the sport-field, the necessary compensations to this routine. The preparation of the soldier, the parade, the smartness and polish of the equipment and uniform, the precise movement of large bodies of men, the blare of bugles, the punctuation of drums, the rhythm of the march, and then, in actual battle itself, the final explosion of effort in the bombardment and the charge, lend an esthetic and moral grandeur to the whole performance. The death or maiming of the body gives the drama the element of a tragic sacrifice, like that which underlies so many primitive religious rituals: the effort is sanctified and intensified by the scale of the holocaust. For peoples that have lost the values of culture and can no longer respond with interest or understanding to the symbols of culture, the abandonment of the whole process and the reversion to crude faiths and non-rational dogmas, is powerfully abetted by the processes of war. If no enemy really existed, it would be necessary to create him, in order to further this development.

Thus war breaks the tedium of a mechanized society and relieves it from the pettiness and prudence of its daily efforts, by concentrating to their last degree both the mechanization of the means of production and the countering vigor of desperate vital outbursts. War sanctions the utmost exhibition of the primitive at the same time that it deifies the mechanical. In modern war, the raw primitive and the clockwork mechanical are one.

In view of its end products—the dead, the crippled, the insane, the devastated regions, the shattered resources, the moral corruption, the anti-social hates and hoodlumisms—war is the most disastrous outlet for the repressed impulses of society that has been devised. The evil consequences have increased in magnitude and in human distress in proportion as the actual elements of fighting have become more mechanized: the threat of chemical warfare against the civilian population as well as the military arm places in the hands of the armies of the world instruments of ruthlessness of which only the most savage conquerors in the past would have taken advantage. The difference between the Athenians with their swords and shields fighting on the fields of Marathon, and the soldiers who faced each other with tanks, guns, flame-throwers, poison gases, and hand-grenades on the Western Front, is the difference between the ritual of the dance and the routine of the slaughter house. One is an exhibition of skill and courage with the chance of death present, the other is an exhibition of the arts of death, with the almost accidental by-product of skill and courage. But it is in death that these repressed and regimented populations have their first glimpse of effective life; and the cult of death is a sign of their throwback to the corrupt primitive.

As a back-fire against mechanism, war, even more than mass-sport, has increased the area of the conflagration without stemming its advance. Still, as long as the machine remains an absolute, war will represent for this society the sum of its values and compensations: for war brings people back to the earth, makes them face the battle with the elements, unleashes the brute forces of their own nature, releases the normal restraints of social life, and sanctions a return to the primitive in thought and feeling, even as it further sanctions infantility in the blind personal obedience it exacts, like that of the archetypal father with the archetypal son, which divests the latter of the need of behaving like a responsible and autonomous personality. Savagery, which we have associated with the not-yet-civilized, is equally a reversionary mode that arises with the mechanically over-civilized. Sometimes the mechanism against which reaction takes place is a compulsive morality or social regimentation: in the case of Western peoples it is the too-closely regimented environment we associate with the machine. War, like a neurosis, is the destructive solution of an unbearable tension and conflict between organic impulses and the code and circumstances that keep one from satisfying them.

This destructive union of the mechanized and the savage primitive is the alternative to a mature, humanized culture capable of directing the machine to the enhancement of communal and personal life. If our life were an organic whole this split and this perversion would not be possible, for the order we have embodied in machines would be more completely exemplified in our personal life, and the primitive impulses, which we have diverted or repressed by excessive preoccupation with mechanical devices, would have natural outlets in their appropriate cultural forms. Until we begin to achieve this culture, however, war will probably remain the constant shadow of the machine: the wars of national armies, the wars of gangs, the wars of classes: beneath all, the incessant preparation by drill and propaganda towards these wars. A society that has lost its life values will tend to make a religion of death and build up a cult around its worship—a religion not less grateful because it satisfies the mounting number of paranoiacs and sadists such a disrupted society necessarily produces.

12: The Minor Shock-Absorbers

From all the forms of resistance and compensation we have been examining it is plain that the introduction of the machine was not smooth, nor were its characteristic habits of life undisputed. The

reactions would probably have been more numerous and more decisive had it not been for the fact that old habits of thought and old
ways of life continued in existence: this bridged the gap between the
old and the new, and kept the machine from dominating life as a
whole as much as it controlled the routine of industrial activity.
In part, these existing institutions, while they stabilized society, prevented it from absorbing and reacting upon the cultural elements
derived from the machine: so that they lessened the valuable offices
of the machine in the act of mitigating its defects.

In addition to the stabilizing inertia of society as a whole, and to
the many-sided attempts to combat the machine by the force of ideas
and institutional contrivances, there were still other reactions that
served, as it were, as cushions and shock-absorbers. So far from
stopping the machine or undermining the purely mechanical program, they perhaps decreased the tensions that the machine produced.
Thus the tendency to destroy the memorials of older cultures, exhibited by the utilitarians in their first vigor of self-confidence and
creative effort, was met in part among the very classes that were most
active in this attack, by the cult of antiquarianism.

This cult lacked the passionate conviction that one period or another of the past was of supreme value: it merely held that almost
anything old was *ipso facto* valuable or beautiful, whether it was
a fragment of Roman statuary, a wooden image of a fifteenth century
saint, or an iron door knocker. The exponents of this cult attempted
to create private environments from which every hint of the machine
was absent: they burned wooden logs in the open fireplaces of imitation Norman manor houses, which were in reality heated by steam,
designed with the help of a camera and measured drawings, and
supported, where the architect was a little uncertain of his skill
or materials, with concealed steel beams. When handicraft articles
could not be filched from the decayed buildings of the past, they
were copied with vast effort by belated handworkers: when the demand for such copies filtered down through the middle classes, they
were then reproduced by means of power machinery in a fashion
capable of deceiving only the blind and ignorant: a double prevari-
cation.

Oppressed by a mechanical environment they had neither mastered nor humanized nor succeeded esthetically in appreciating, the ruling classes and their imitators among the lesser bourgeoisie retreated from the factory or the office into a fake non-mechanical environment, in which the past was modified by the addition of physical comforts, such as tropical temperature in the winter, and springs and padding on sofas, lounges, beds. Each successful individual produced his own special antiquarian environment: a private world.

This private world, as lived in Suburbia or in the more palatial country houses, is not to be differentiated by any objective standard from the world in which the lunatic attempts to live out the drama in which he appears to himself to be Lorenzo the Magnificent or Louis XIV. In each case the difficulty of maintaining an equilibrium in relation to a difficult or hostile external world is solved by withdrawal, permanent or temporary, into a private retreat, untainted by most of the conditions that public life and effort lay down. These antiquarian stage-settings, which characterized for the most part the domestic equipment of the more successful members of the bourgeoisie from the eighteenth century onward—with a minor interlude of self-confident ugliness during the high paleotechnic period— these stage-settings were, on a strict psychological interpretation, cells: indeed, the addition of "comforts" made them padded cells. Those who lived in them were stable, "normal," "adjusted" people. In relation to the entire environment in which they worked and thought and lived, they merely behaved *as if* they were in a state of neurotic collapse, *as if* there were a deep conflict between their inner drive and the mechanical environment they had helped to create, *as if* they had been unable to resolve their divided activities into a single consistent pattern.

The other side of this conservatism of taste and this refusal to recognize natural change was the tendency to take refuge in change for its own sake, and to hasten the very process that was introduced by the machine. Changing the style of an object, altering its superficial shape or color, without effecting any real improvement, became part of the routine of modern society just because the natural variations and breaks in life were absent: the answer to excessive regimentation came in through an equally heightened and over-stimulated demand for novelties. In the long run, unceasing change is as monotonous as unceasing sameness: real refreshment implies both uncertainty and choice, and to have to abandon choice merely because for external reasons a style has changed is to forfeit what real gain has been made. Here again change and novelty are no more sacred, no more inimical, than stability and monotony: but the purposeless materialism and imbecile regimentation of production resulted in the aimless change and the absence of real stimuli and effective adjustments in consumption; and so far from resolving the difficulty the resistance only increased it. The itch for change: the itch for movement: the itch for novelty infected the entire system of production and consumption and severed them from the real standards and norms which it was highly important to devise. When people's work and days were varied they were content to remain in the same place; when their lives were ironed out into a blank routine they found it necessary to move; and the more rapidly they moved the more standardized became the environment in which they moved: there was no getting away from it. So it went in every department of life.

Where the physical means of withdrawal were inadequate, pure fantasy flourished without any other external means than the word or the picture. But these external means were put upon a mechanized collective basis during the nineteenth century, as a result of the cheapened processes of production made possible by the rotary press, the camera, photo-engraving, and the motion picture. With the spread of literacy, literature of all grades and levels formed a semi-public world into which the unsatisfied individual might withdraw, to live a life of adventure following the travellers and explorers in their memoirs, to live a life of dangerous action and keen observation by participating in the crimes and investigations of a Dupin or a Sherlock Holmes, or to live a life of romantic fulfillment in the love stories and erotic romances that became everyone's property from the eighteenth century onward. Most of these varieties of day-dream and private fantasy had of course existed in the past: now they became part of a gigantic collective apparatus of escape. So important was the function of popular literature as escape that many modern psychologists have treated literature as a whole as a mere vehicle of withdrawal from the harsh realities of existence: forgetful of the fact that literature of the first order, so far from being a mere pleasure-device, is a supreme attempt to face and encompass reality—an attempt beside which a busy working life involves a shrinkage and represents a partial retreat.

During the nineteenth century vulgar literature to a large extent replaced the mythological constructions of religion: the austere cosmical sweep and the careful moral codes of the more sacred religions were, alas! a little too much akin to the machine itself, from which people were trying to escape. This withdrawal into fantasy was immensely re-enforced from 1910 on, by the motion-picture, which came into existence just when the pressure from the machine was beginning to bear down more and more inexorably. Public daydreams of wealth, magnificence, adventure, irregularity and spontaneous action—identification with the criminal defying the forces of order—identification with the courtesan practicing openly the allurements of sex—these scarcely adolescent fantasies, created and projected with the aid of the machine, made the machine-ritual tolerable to the vast urban or urbanized populations of the world. But these dreams were no longer private, and what is more they were no longer spontaneous and free: they were promptly capitalized on a vast scale as the "amusement business," and established as a vested interest. To create a more liberal life that might do without such anodynes was to threaten the safety of investments, built on the certainty of continued dullness, boredom and defeat.

Too dull to think, people might read: too tired to read, they might look at the moving pictures: unable to visit the picture theater they might turn on the radio: in any case, they might avoid the call to action: surrogate lovers, surrogate heroes and heroines, surrogate wealth filled their debilitated and impoverished lives and carried the perfume of unreality into their dwellings. And as the machine itself became, as it were, more active and human, reproducing the organic properties of eye and ear, the human beings who employed the machine as a mode of escape have tended to become more passive and mechanical. Unsure of their own voices, unable to hold a tune, they carry a phonograph or a radio set with them even on a picnic: afraid to be alone with their own thoughts, afraid to confront the blankness and inertia of their own minds, they turn on the radio and eat and talk and sleep to the accompaniment of a continuous stimulus from the outside world: now a band, now a bit of propaganda, now a piece of public gossip called news. Even such autonomy as the poorest drudge once had, left like Cinderella to her dreams of Prince Charming when her sisters went off to the ball, is gone in this mechanical environment: whatever compensations her present-day counterpart may have, it must come through the machine. Using the machine alone to escape from the machine, our mechanized populations have jumped from a hot frying pan into a hotter fire. The shock-absorbers are of the same order as the environment itself. The moving picture deliberately glorifies the cold brutality and homicidal lusts of gangsterdom: the newsreel prepares for battles to come by exhibiting each week the latest devices of armed combat, accompanied by a few persuasive bars from the national anthem. In the act of relieving psychological strain these various devices only increase the final tension and support more disastrous forms of release. After one has lived through a thousand callous deaths on the screen one is ready for a rape, a lynching, a murder, or a war in actual life: when the surrogate excitements of the film and the radio begin to pall, a taste of real blood becomes necessary. In short: the shock-absorber prepares one for a fresh shock.

13: Resistance and Adjustment

In all these efforts to attack, to resist, or to retreat from the machine the observer may be tempted to see nothing more than the phenomenon that Professor W. F. Ogburn has described as the "cultural lag." The failure of "adjustment" may be looked upon as a failure of art and morals and religion to change with the same degree of rapidity as the machine and to change in the same direction.

This seems to me an essentially superficial interpretation. For one thing, change in a direction *opposite* to the machine may be as important in ensuring adjustment as change in the same direction, when it happens that the machine is taking a course that would,

unless compensated, lead to human deterioration and collapse. For
another thing, this interpretation regards the machine as an independent structure, and it holds the direction and rate of change
assumed by the machine as a norm, to which all the other aspects of·
human life must conform. In truth, interactions between organisms
and their environments take place in both directions, and it is just
as correct to regard the machinery of warfare as retarded in relation
to the morality of Confucius as to take the opposite position. In his
The Instinct of Workmanship Thorstein Veblen carefully avoided
the one-sided notion of adjustment: but later economists and sociolo-
gists have not always been so unparochial, and they have treated the
machine as if it were final and as if it were something other than the
projection of one particular side of the human personality.

All the arts and institutions of man derive their authority from
the nature of human life as such. This applies as fully to technics
as to painting. A particular economic or technical régime may deny
this nature, as some particular social custom, like that of binding
the feet of women or enforcing virginity, may deny the patent facts
of physiology and anatomy: but such erroneous views and usages
do not eliminate the fact they deny. At all events, the mere bulk of
technology, its mere power and ubiquitousness, give no proof whatever of its relative human value or its place in the economy of an
intelligent human society. The very fact that one encounters resistances, reversions, archaicisms at the moment of the greatest technical
achievement—even among those classes who have, from the standpoint of wealth and power, benefited most by the victory of the
machine—makes one doubt both the effectiveness and the sufficiency
of the whole scheme of life the machine has so far brought into
existence. And who is so innocent today as to think that maladjust-
ment to the machine can be solved by the simple process of introducing greater quantities of machinery?

Plainly, if human life consisted solely in adjustment to the dominant physical and social environment, man would have left the
world as he found it, as most of his biological companions have done:
the machine itself would not have been invented. Man's singular
ability consists in the fact that he creates standards and ends of his

own, not given directly in the external scheme of things, and in ful-
filling his own nature in cooperation with the environment, he creates
a third realm, the realm of the arts, in which the two are harmonized
and ordered and made significant. Man is that part of nature in
which causality may, under appropriate circumstances, give place to
finality: in which the ends condition the means. Sometimes man's
standards are grotesque and arbitrary: untempered by positive
knowledge and a just sense of his limitations, man is capable of
deforming the human anatomy in pursuit of a barbarous dream of
beauty, or, to objectify his fears and his tortured desires, he may
resort to horrible human sacrifices. But even in these perversions
there is an acknowledgment that man himself in part creates the
conditions under which he lives, and is not merely the impotent
prisoner of circumstances.

If this has been man's attitude toward Nature, why should he
assume a more craven posture in confronting the machine, whose
physical laws he discovered, whose body he created, whose rhythms
he anticipated by external feats of regimentation in his own life?
It is absurd to hold that we must continue to accept the bourgeoisie's
overwhelming concern for power, practical success, above all for
comfort, or that we must passively absorb, without discrimination
and selection—which implies, where necessary, rejection—all the
new products of the machine. It is equally foolish to believe that we
must conform our living and thinking to the antiquated ideological
system which helped create the numerous brilliant short cuts that
attended the early development of the machine. The real question
before us lies here: do these instruments further life and enhance
its values, or not? Some of the results, as I shall show in the next
chapter, are admirable, far more admirable even than the inventor
and the industrialist and the utilitarian permitted himself to imagine.
Other aspects of the machine are on the contrary trifling, and still
others, like modern mechanized warfare, are deliberately antag-
onistic to every ideal of humanity—even to the old-fashioned ideal
of the soldier who once risked his life in equal combat. In these latter
cases, our problem is to eliminate or subjugate the machine, unless
we ourselves wish to be eliminated. For it is not automatism and

standardization and order that are dangerous: what is dangerous is the restriction of life that has so often attended their untutored acceptance. By what inept logic must we bow to our creation if it be a machine, and spurn it as "unreal" if it happens to be a painting or a poem? The machine is just as much a creature of thought as the poem: the poem is as much a fact of reality as the machine. Those who use the machine when they need to react to life directly or employ the humane arts, are as completely lacking in efficiency as if they studied metaphysics in order to learn how to bake bread. The question in each case is: what is the appropriate life-reaction? How far does this or that instrument further the biological purposes or the ideal ends of life?

Every form of life, as Patrick Geddes has expressed it, is marked not merely by adjustment to the environment, but by insurgence against the environment: it is both creature and creator, both the victim of fate and the master of destiny: it lives no less by domination than by acceptance. In man this insurgence reaches its apex, and manifests itself most completely, perhaps, in the arts, where dream and actuality, the imagination and its limiting conditions, the ideal and the means, are fused together in the dynamic act of expression and in the resultant body that is expressed. As a being with a social heritage, man belongs to a world that includes the past and the future, in which he can by his selective efforts create passages and ends not derived from the immediate situation, and alter the blind direction of the senseless forces that surround him.

To recognize these facts is perhaps the first step toward dealing rationally with the machine. We must abandon our futile and lamentable dodges for resisting the machine by stultifying relapses into savagery, by recourse to anesthetics and shock-absorbers. Though they temporarily may relieve the strain, in the end they do more harm than they avoid. On the other hand, the most objective advocates of the machine must recognize the underlying human validity of the Romantic protest against the machine: the elements originally embodied in literature and art in the romantic movement are essential parts of the human heritage that can not be neglected or flouted: they point to a synthesis more comprehensive than that developed through the organs of the machine itself. Failing to create this synthesis, failing to incorporate it in our personal and communal life, the machine will be able to continue only with the aid of shock-absorbers which confirm its worst characteristics, or with the compensatory adjustment of vicious and barbaric elements which will, in all probability, ruin the entire structure of our civilization.

II
ASSIMILATION OF THE MACHINE

1: New Cultural Values

The tools and utensils used during the greater part of man's history were, in the main, extensions of his own organism: they did not have—what is more important they did not *seem* to have—an independent existence. But though they were an intimate part of the worker, they reacted upon his capacities, sharpening his eye, refining his skill, teaching him to respect the nature of the material with which he was dealing. The tool brought man into closer harmony with his environment, not merely because it enabled him to re-shape it, but because it made him recognize the limits of his capacities. In dream, he was all powerful: in reality he had to recognize the weight of stone and cut stones no bigger than he could transport. In the book of wisdom the carpenter, the smith, the potter, the peasant wrote, if they did not sign, their several pages. And in this sense, technics has been, in every age, a constant instrument of discipline and education. A surviving primitive might, here and there, vent his anger on a cart that got stuck in the mud by breaking up its wheels, in the same fashion that he would beat a donkey that refused to move: but the mass of mankind learned, at least during the period of the written record, that certain parts of the environment can neither be intimidated nor cajoled. To control them, one must learn the laws of their behavior, instead of petulantly imposing one's own wishes. Thus the lore and tradition of technics, however empirical, tended to create the picture of an objective reality. Something of this fact remained in the Victorian definition of science as "organized common sense."

Because of their independent source of power, and their semi-automatic operation even in their cruder forms, machines have seemed to have a reality and an independent existence apart from the user. Whereas the educational values of handicraft were mainly in the process, those of the machine were largely in the preparatory design: hence the process itself was understood only by the machinists and technicians responsible for the design and operation of the actual machinery. As production became more mechanized and the discipline of the factory became more impersonal and the work itself became less rewarding, apart from such slight opportunities for social intercourse as it furthered, attention was centered more and more upon the product: people valued the machine for its external achievements, for the number of yards of cloth it wove, for the number of miles it carried them. The machine thus appeared purely as an external instrument for the conquest of the environment: the actual forms of the products, the actual collaboration and intelligence manifested in creating them, the educational possibilities of this impersonal cooperation itself—all these elements were neglected. We assimilated the objects rather than the spirit that produced them, and so far from respecting that spirit, we again and again attempted to make the objects themselves seem to be something other than a product of the machine. We did not expect beauty through the machine any more than we expected a higher standard of morality from the laboratory: yet the fact remains that if we seek an authentic sample of a new esthetic or a higher ethic during the nineteenth century it is in technics and science that we will perhaps most easily find them.

The practical men themselves were the very persons who stood in the way of our recognizing that the significance of the machine was not limited to its practical achievements. For, on the terms that the inventors and industrialists considered the machine, it did not carry over from the factory and the marketplace into any other department of human life, except as a means. The possibility that technics had become a creative force, carried on by its own momentum, that it was rapidly ordering a new kind of environment and was producing a third estate midway between nature and the humane arts, that it was not merely a quicker way of achieving old ends but an effective way of expressing new ends—the possibility in short that the machine furthered a new mode of *living* was far from the minds of those who actively promoted it. The industrialists and engineers themselves did not believe in the qualitative and cultural aspects of the machine. In their indifference to these aspects, they were just as far from appreciating the nature of the machine as were the Romantics: only what the Romantics, judging the machine from the standpoint of life, regarded as a defect the utilitarian boasted of as a virtue: for the latter the absence of art was an assurance of practicality.

If the machine had really lacked cultural values, the Romantics would have been right, and their desire to seek these values, if need be, in a dead past would have been justified by the very desperateness of the case. But the interests in the factual and the practical, which the industrialist made the sole key to intelligence, were only two in a whole series of new values that had been called into existence by the development of the new technics. Matters of fact and practice had usually in previous civilizations been treated with snobbish contempt by the leisured classes: as if the logical ordering of propositions were any nobler a technical feat than the articulation of machines. The interest in the practical was symptomatic of that wider and more intelligible world in which people had begun to live, a world in which the taboos of class and caste could no longer be considered as definitive in dealing with events and experiences. Capitalism and technics had both acted as a solvent of these clots of prejudice and intellectual confusion; and they were thus at first important liberators of life.

From the beginning, indeed, the most durable conquests of the machine lay not in the instruments themselves, which quickly became outmoded, nor in the goods produced, which quickly were consumed, but in the modes of life made possible via the machine and in the machine: the cranky mechanical slave was also a pedagogue. While the machine increased the servitude of servile personalities, it also promised the further liberation of released personalities: it challenged thought and effort as no previous system of technics had done. No part of the environment, no social conventions, could be taken for granted, once the machine had shown how far order and system and intelligence might prevail over the raw nature of things.

What remains as the permanent contribution of the machine, carried over from one generation to another, is the technique of cooperative thought and action it has fostered, the esthetic excellence of the machine forms, the delicate logic of materials and forces, which has added a new canon—the machine canon—to the arts: above all, perhaps, the more objective personality that has come into existence through a more sensitive and understanding intercourse with these new social instruments and through their deliberate cultural assimilation. *In projecting one side of the human personality into the concrete forms of the machine, we have created an independent environment that has reacted upon every other side of the personality.*

In the past, the irrational and demonic aspects of life had invaded spheres where they did not belong. It was a step in advance to discover that bacteria, not brownies, were responsible for curdling milk, and that an air-cooled motor was more effective than a witch's broomstick for rapid long distance transportation. This triumph of order was pervasive: it gave a confidence to human purposes akin to that which a well-drilled regiment has when it marches in step. Creating the illusion of invincibility, the machine actually added to the amount of power man can exercize. Science and technics stiffened our morale: by their very austerities and abnegations they enhanced the value of the human personality that submitted to their discipline: they cast contempt on childish fears, childish guesses, equally childish assertions. By means of the machine man gave a concrete and external and impersonal form to his desire for order: and in a subtle way he thus set a new standard for his personal life and his more organic attitudes. Unless he was better than the machine he would only find himself reduced to its level: dumb, servile, abject, a creature of immediate reflexes and passive unselective responses.

While many of the boasted achievements of industrialism are merely rubbish, and while many of the goods produced by the machine are fraudulent and evanescent, its esthetic, its logic, and its factual technique remain a durable contribution: they are among man's supreme conquests. The practical results may be admirable or dubious: but the method that underlies them has a permanent importance to the race, apart from its immediate consequences. For the machine has added a whole series of arts to those produced by simple tools and handicraft methods and it has added a new realm to the environment in which the cultured man works and feels and thinks. Similarly, it has extended the power and range of human organs and has disclosed new esthetic spectacles, new worlds. The exact arts produced with the aid of the machine have their proper standards and give their own peculiar satisfactions to the human spirit. Differing in technique from the arts of the past, they spring nevertheless from the same source: for the machine itself, I must stress for the tenth time, is a human product, and its very abstractions make it more definitely human in one sense than those humane arts which on occasion realistically counterfeit nature.

Here, beyond what appears at the moment of realization, is the vital contribution of the machine. What matters the fact that the ordinary workman has the equivalent of 240 slaves to help him, if the master himself remains an imbecile, devouring the spurious news, the false suggestions, the intellectual prejudices that play upon him in the press and the school, giving vent in turn to tribal assertions and primitive lusts under the impression that he is the final token of progress and civilization. One does not make a child powerful by placing a stick of dynamite in his hands: one only adds to the dangers of his irresponsibility. Were mankind to remain children, they would exercize more effective power by being reduced to using a lump of clay and an old-fashioned modelling tool. But if the machine is one of the aids man has created toward achieving further intellectual growth and attaining maturity, if he treats this powerful automaton of his as a challenge to his own development, if the exact arts fostered by the machine have their own contribution to make to the mind, and are aids in the orderly crystallization of experience, then these contributions are vital ones indeed. The machine, which reached such overwhelming dimensions in Western Civilization partly because it sprang out of a disrupted and one-sided culture, nevertheless may help in enlarging the provinces of culture itself and thereby in building a greater synthesis: in that case, it will carry an antidote to its own poison. So let us consider the machine more closely as. an instrument of culture and examine the ways in which we have begun, during the last century, to assimilate it.

2: The Neutrality of Order

Before the machine pervaded life, order was the boast of the gods and absolute monarchs. Both the deity and his representatives on earth had, however, the misfortune to be inscrutable in their judgment and frequently capricious and cruel in their assertion of mastery. On the human level, their order was represented by slavery: complete determination from above: complete subservience without question or understanding below. Behind the gods and the absolute monarchs stood brute nature itself, filled with demons, djinns, trolls, giants, contesting the reign of the gods. Chance and the accidental malice of the universe cut across the purposes of men and the observable regularities of nature. Even as a symbol the absolute monarch was weak as an exponent of order: his troops might obey with absolute precision, but he might be undone, as Hans Andersen pointed out in one of his fairy tales, by the small torture of a gnat.

With the development of the sciences and with the articulation of the machine in practical life, the realm of order was transferred from the absolute rulers, exercizing a personal control, to the universe of impersonal nature and to the particular group of artifacts and customs we call the machine. The royal formula of purpose—"I will"—was translated into the causal terms of science—"It must." By partly supplanting the crude desire for personal dominion by an impersonal curiosity and by the desire to understand, science prepared the way for a more effective conquest of the external environment and ultimately for a more effective control of the agent, man, himself. That a part of the order of the universe was a contribution by man himself, that the limitations imposed upon scientific research by human instruments and interests tend to produce an orderly and mathematically analyzable result, does not lessen the wonder and the beauty of the system: it rather gives to the conception of the universe itself some of the character of a work of art. To acknowledge the limitations imposed by science, to subordinate the wish to the fact, and to look for order as an emergent in observed relations, rather than as an extraneous scheme imposed upon these relations— these were the great contributions of the new outlook on life. Expressing regularities and recurrent series, science widened the area of certainty, prediction, and control.

By deliberately cutting off certain phases of man's personality, the warm life of private sensation and private feelings and private perceptions, the sciences assisted in building up a more public world which gained in accessibility what it lost in depth. To measure a weight, a distance, a charge of electricity, by reference to pointer readings established within a mechanical system, deliberately constructed for this purpose, was to limit the possibility of errors of interpretation, and cancel out the differences of individual experience and private history. And the greater the degree of abstraction and limitation, the greater was the accuracy of reference. By isolating simple systems and simple causal sequences the sciences created confidence in the possibility of finding a similar type of order in every aspect of experience: it was, indeed, by the success of science in the realm of the inorganic that we have acquired whatever belief we may legitimately entertain in the possibility of achieving similar understanding and control in the vastly more complex domain of life.

The first steps in the physical sciences did not go very far. Compared to organic behavior, in which any one of a given set of stimuli may create the same reaction, or in which a single stimulus may under different conditions create a number of different reactions, in which the organism as a whole responds and changes at the same time as the isolated part one seeks to investigate, compared to behavior within this frame the most complicated physical reaction is gratifyingly simple. But the point is that by means of the analyses and instruments developed in the physical sciences and embodied in technics, some of the necessary preliminary instruments for biological and social exploration have been created. All measurement involves the reference of certain parts of a complex phenomenon to a simpler one whose characteristics are relatively independent and fixed and determinable. The whole personality was a useless instrument for investigating limited mechanical phenomena. In its uncritical state, it was likewise useless for investigating organic systems, whether they were animal organisms or social groups. By a process of dismemberment science created a more useful type of order: an order external to the self. In the long run that special limitation fortified the ego as perhaps no other achievement in thought had done.

Although the most intense applications of the scientific method were in technology, the interests that it satisfied and re-excited, the desire for order that it expressed, translated themselves in other spheres. More and more factual research, the document, the exact calculation became a preliminary to expression. Indeed, the respect for quantities became a new condition of what had hitherto been crude qualitative judgments. Good and bad, beauty and ugliness, are determined, not merely by their respective natures but by the quantity one may assign to them in any particular situation. To think closely with respect to quantities is to think more accurately about the essential nature and the actual functions of things: arsenic is a tonic in grains and a poison in ounces: the quantity, the local composition, and the environmental relation of a quality are as important, so to say, as its original sign *as quality*. It is for this reason that a whole series of ethical distinctions, based upon the notion of pure and absolute qualities without relation to their amounts, has been instinctively discarded by a considerable part of mankind: while Samuel Butler's dictum, that every virtue should be mixed with a little of its opposite, implying as it does that qualities are altered by their quantitative relations, seems much closer to the heart of the matter. This respect for quantity has been grossly caricatured by dull pedantic minds who have sought by mathematical means to eliminate the qualitative aspects of complicated social and esthetic situations: but one need not be led by their mistake into failing to recognize the peculiar contribution that our quantitative technique has made in departments apparently remote from the machine.

One must distinguish between the cult of Nature as a standard and a criterion of human expression and the general influence of the scientific spirit. As for the first, one may say that though Ruskin, an esthetic disciple of science, rejected the Greek fret in decoration because it had no counterpart among flowers, minerals, or animals, for us today nature is no longer an absolute: or rather, we no longer regard nature as if man himself were not implicated in her, and as if his modifications of nature were not themselves a part of the natural order to which he is born. Even when emphasizing the impersonality of the machine one must not forget the busy humanizing that goes on before man even half completes his picture of an objective and indifferent nature. All the tools man uses, his eyes with their limited field of vision and their insensitiveness to ultra-violet and infra-red rays, his hands which can hold and manipulate only a limited number of objects at one time, his mind which tends to create categories of twos and threes because, without intensive training, to hold as many ideas together as a musician can hold notes of the piano puts an excessive strain upon his intelligence—still more his microscopes and balances, all bear the imprint of his own character as well as the general characteristics imposed by the physical environment. It has only been by a process of reasoning and inference—itself not free from the taint of his origin—that man has established the neutral realm of nature. Man may arbitrarily define nature as that part of his experience which is neutral to his desires and interests: but he with his desires and interests, to say nothing of his chemical constitution, has been formed by nature and inescapably is part of the system of nature. Once he has picked and chosen from this realm, as he does in science, the result is a work of art—*his* art: certainly it is no longer in a state of nature.

In so far as the cult of nature has made men draw upon a wider experience, to discover themselves in hitherto unexplored environments, and to contrive new isolations in the laboratory which will enable them to make further discoveries, it has been a good influence: man should be at home among the stars as well as at his own fireside. But although the new canon of order has a deep esthetic as well as an intellectual status, external nature has no finally independent authority: it exists, as a result of man's collective experience, and as a subject for his further improvisations by means of science, technics, and the humane arts.

The merit of the new order was to give man by projection an outer world which helped him to make over the hot spontaneous

world of desire he carried within. But the new order, the new impersonality, was but a fragment transplanted from the personality as a
whole: it had existed as part of man before he cut it off and gave
it an independent milieu and an independent root system. The comprehension and transformation of this impersonal "external" world
of technics was one of the great revelations of the painters and artists
and poets of the last three centuries. Art is the re-enactment of reality,
of a reality purified, freed from constraints and irrelevant accidents,
unfettered to the material circumstances that confuse the essence.
The passage of the machine into art was in itself a signal of release—
a sign that the hard necessities of practice, the preoccupation with the
immediate battle was over—a sign that the mind was free once more
to see, to contemplate, and so to enlarge and deepen all the practical
benefits of the machine.

Science had something other to contribute to the arts than the
notion that the machine was an absolute. It contributed, through
its effects upon invention and mechanization, a new type of order to
the environment: an order in which power, economy, objectivity,
the collective will play a more decisive part than they had played
before even in such absolute forms of dominion as in the royal
priesthood—and engineers—of Egypt or Babylon. The sensitive
apprehension of this new environment, its translation into terms
which involve human affections and feelings, and that bring into
play once more the full personality, became part of the mission of
the artist: and the great spirits of the nineteenth century, who first
fully greeted this altered environment, were not indifferent to it.
Turner and Tennyson, Emily Dickinson and Thoreau, Whitman and
Emerson, all saluted with admiration the locomotive, that symbol
of the new order in Western Society. They were conscious of the fact
that new instruments were changing the dimensions and to some
extent therefore the very qualities of experience; these facts were
just as clear to Thoreau as to Samuel Smiles; to Kipling as to H. G.
Wells. The telegraph wire, the locomotive, the ocean steamship, the
very shafts and pistons and switches that conveyed and canalized or
controlled the new power, could awaken emotion as well as the harp

and the war-horse: the hand at the throttle or the switch was no less regal than the hand that had once held a scepter.

The second contribution of the scientific attitude was a limiting one: it tended to destroy the lingering mythologies of Greek goddesses and Christian heroes and saints; or rather, it prevented a naive and repetitious use of these symbols. But at the same time, it disclosed new universal symbols, and widened the very domain of the symbol itself. This process took place in all the arts: it affected poetry as well as architecture. The pursuit of science, however, suggested new myths. The transformation of the medieval folk-legend of Dr. Faustus from Marlowe to Goethe, with Faust ending up as a builder of canals and a drainer of swamps and finding the meaning of life in sheer activity, the transformation of the Prometheus myth in Melville's Moby Dick, testify not to the destruction of myths by positive knowledge but to their more pregnant application. I can only repeat here what I have said in another place: "What the scientific spirit has actually done has been to exercise the imagination in finer ways than the autistic wish—the wish of the infant possessed of the illusions of power and domination—was able to express. Faraday's ability to conceive the lines of force in a magnetic field was quite as great a triumph as the ability to conceive of fairies dancing in a ring: and, Mr. A. N. Whitehead has shown, the poets who sympathized with this new sort of imagination, poets like Shelley, Wordsworth, Whitman, Melville, did not feel themselves robbed of their specific powers, but rather found them enlarged and refreshed.

"One of the finest love poems in the nineteenth century, Whitman's Out of the Cradle Endlessly Rocking, is expressed in such an image as Darwin or Audubon might have used, were the scientist as capable of expressing his inner feelings as of noting 'external' events: the poet haunting the seashore and observing the mating of the birds, day after day following their life, could scarcely have existed before the nineteenth century. In the early seventeenth century such a poet would have remained in the garden and written about a literary ghost, Philomel, and not about an actual pair of birds; in Pope's time the poet would have remained in the library and written about the birds on a lady's fan. Almost all the important works of the nineteenth century were cast in this mode and expressed the new imaginative range: they respect the fact: they are replete with observation: they project an ideal realm in and through, not transcendentally over, the landscape of actuality. Notre Dame might have been written by an historian, War and Peace by a sociologist, The Idiot might have been created by a psychiatrist, and Salammbô might have been the work of an archaeologist. I do not say that these books were scientific by intention, or that they might be replaced by a work of science without grave loss; far from it. I merely point out that they were conceived in the same spirit; that they belong to a similar plane of consciousness."

Once the symbol was focussed, the task of the practical arts became more purposive. Science gave the artist and the technician new objectives: it demanded that he respond to the nature of the machine's functions and refrain from seeking to express his personality by irrelevant and surreptitious means upon the objective material. The woodiness of wood, the glassiness of glass, the metallic quality of steel, the movement of motion—these attributes had been analyzed out by chemical and physical means, and to respect them was to understand and work with the new environment. Ornament, conceived apart from function, was as barbarous as the tattooing of the human body: the naked object, whatever it was, had its own beauty, whose revealment made it more human, and more close to the new personality than could any amount of artful decoration. While the Dutch gardeners of the seventeenth century had often, for example, turned the privet and the box into the shapes of animals and arbitrary figures, a new type of gardening appeared in the twentieth century which respected the natural ecological partnerships, and which not merely permitted plants to grow in their natural shapes but sought simply to clarify their natural relationships: scientific knowledge was one of the facts that indirectly contributed to the esthetic pleasure. That change symbolizes what has been steadily happening, sometimes slowly, sometimes rapidly, in all the arts. For finally, if nature itself is not an absolute, and if the facts of external nature are not the artist's sole materials, nor its literal imitation his guarantee of esthetic success, science nevertheless gives him the assurance of a partly independent realm which defines the limits of his own working powers. In creating his union of the inner world and the outer, of his passions and affections with the thing that exists, the artist need not remain the passive victim of his neurotic caprices and hallucinations: hence even when he departs from some external objective form or some tried convention, he still has a common measure of the extent of his deviation. While the determinism of the object—if one may coin a phrase—is more emphatic in the mechanical arts than in the humane ones, a binding thread runs through both realms.

Co-ordinate with the intellectual assimilation of the machine by the technician and the artist, which came partly through habit, partly through workaday experience, and partly through the extension of systematic training in science, came the esthetic and emotional apprehension of the new environment. Let us consider this in detail.

3: The Esthetic Experience of the Machine

The developed environment of the machine in the twentieth century has its kinship with primitive approximations to this order in the castles and fortifications and bridges from the eleventh to the thirteenth centuries, and even later: the bridge at Tournay or the brickwork and vaults of the Marienkirche at Lübeck: these earliest touches of the practical have the same fine characteristics that the latest grain elevators or steel cranes have. But the new characteristics now touch almost every department of experience. Observe the derricks, the ropes, the stanchions and ladders of a modern steamship, close at hand in the night, when the hard shadows mingle obliquely with the hard white shapes. Here is a new fact of esthetic experience; and it must be transposed in the same hard way: to look for gradation and atmosphere here is to miss a fresh quality that has emerged through the use of mechanical forms and mechanical modes of lighting. Or stand on a deserted subway platform and contemplate the low cavity becoming a black disc into which, as the train rumbles toward the station, two green circles appear as pin-points widening into plates. Or follow the spidery repetition of boundary lines, defining unoccupied cubes, which make the skeleton of a modern skyscraper: an effect not given even in wood before machine-sawed beams were possible. Or pass along the waterfront in Hamburg, say, and review the line of gigantic steel birds with spread legs that preside over the filling and emptying of the vessels in the basin: that span of legs, that long neck, the play of movement in this vast mechanism, the peculiar pleasure derived from the apparent lightness combined with enormous strength in its working, never existed on this scale in any other environment: compared to these cranes the pyramids of Egypt belong to the order of mud-pies. Or put your eye at the eyepiece of a microscope, and focus the high-powered lens on a thread, a hair, a section of leaf, a drop of blood: here is a world with forms and colors as varied and mysterious as those one finds in the depths of the sea. Or stand in a warehouse and observe a row of bathtubs, a row of siphons, a row of bottles, each of identical size, shape, color, stretching away for a quarter of a mile: the special visual effect of a repeating pattern, exhibited once in great temples or massed armies, is now a commonplace of the mechanical environment. There is an esthetic of units and series, as well as an esthetic of the unique and the non-repeatable.

Absent from such experiences, for the most part, is the play of surfaces, the dance of subtle lights and shadows, the nuances of color, tones, atmosphere, the intricate harmonies that human bodies and specifically organic settings display—all the qualities that belong to the traditional levels of experience and to the unordered world of nature. But face to face with these new machines and instruments, with their hard surfaces, their rigid volumes, their stark shapes, a fresh kind of perception and pleasure emerges: to interpret this order becomes one of the new tasks of the arts. While these new qualities existed as facts of mechanical industry, they were not generally recognized as values until they were interpreted by the painter and the sculptor; and so they existed in an indifferent anonymity for more than a century. The new forms were sometimes appreciated, perhaps, as symbols of Progress: but art, as such, is valued for what it is, not for what it indicates, and the sort of attention needed for the appreciation of art was largely lacking in the industrial environment of the nineteenth century, and except for the work of an occasional engineer of great talent, like Eiffel, was looked upon with deep suspicion.

At the very moment when the praise of industrialism was loudest and most confident, the environment of the machine was regarded as inherently ugly: so ugly that it mattered not how much additional ugliness was created by litter, refuse, slag-piles, scrap metal, or removable dirt. Just as Watt's contemporaries demanded more noise in the steam engine, as a proclamation of power, so did the paleotechnic mind glory, for the most part, in the anti-esthetic quality of the machine.

The Cubists were perhaps the first school to overcome this association of the ugly and the mechanical: they not merely held that beauty could be produced through the machine: they even pointed to the fact that it had been produced. The first expression of Cubism indeed dates back to the seventeenth century: Jean Baptiste Bracelle, in 1624, did a series of Bizarreries which depicted mechanical men, thoroughly cubist in conception. This anticipated in art, as Glanvill did in science, our later interests and inventions. What did the modern Cubists do? They extracted from the organic environment just those elements that could be stated in abstract geometrical symbols: they transposed and readjusted the contents of vision as freely as the inventor readjusted organic functions: they even created on canvas or in metal mechanical equivalents of organic objects: Léger painted human figures that looked as if they had been turned in a lathe, and Duchamp-Villon modeled a horse as if it were a machine. This whole process of rational experiment in abstract mechanical forms was pushed further by the constructivists. Artists like Grabo and Moholy-Nagy put together pieces of abstract sculpture, composed of glass, metal plates, spiral springs, wood, which were the non-utilitarian equivalents of the apparatus that the physical scientist was using in his laboratory. They created in form the semblance of the mathematical equations and physical formulae that had produced our new environment, seeking in this new sculpture to observe the physical laws of equipose or to evolve dynamic equivalents for the solid sculpture of the past by rotating a part of the object through space.

The ultimate worth of such efforts did not perhaps lie in the art itself: for the original machines and instruments were often just as stimulating as their equivalents, and the new pieces of sculpture were just as limited as the machines. No: the worth of these efforts lay in the increased sensitiveness to the mechanical environment that was produced in those who understood and appreciated this art. The esthetic experiment occupied a place comparable to the scientific experiment: it was an attempt to use a certain kind of physical apparatus for the purpose of isolating a phenomenon in experience and for determining the values of certain relations: the experiment was a guide to thought and an approach to action. Like the abstract paintings of Braque, Picasso, Léger, Kandinsky, these constructivist experiments sharpened the response to the machine as an esthetic object. By analyzing, with the aid of simple constructions, the effects produced, they showed what to look for and what values to expect. Calculation, invention, mathematical organization played a special rôle in the new visual effects produced by the machine, while the constant lighting of the sculpture and the canvas, made possible by electricity, profoundly altered the visual relationship. By a process of abstraction the new paintings finally, in some of the painters like Mondrian, approached a purely geometrical formula, with a mere residue of visual content.

Perhaps the most complete as well as the most brilliant interpretations of the capacities of the machine was in the sculpture of Brancusi: for he exhibited both form, method, and symbol. In Brancusi's work one notes first of all the importance of the material, with its specific weight, shape, texture, color, finish: when he models in wood he still endeavors to keep the organic shape of the tree, emphasizing rather than reducing the part given by nature, whereas when he models in marble he brings out to the full the smooth satiny texture, in the smoothest and most egg-like of forms. The respect for material extends further into the conception of the subject treated: the individual is submerged, as in science, into the class: instead of representing in marble the counterfeit head of a mother and child, he lays two blocks of marble side by side with only the faintest depression of surface to indicate the features of the face: it is by relations of volume that he presents the generic idea of mother and child: the idea in its most tenuous form. Again, in his famous bird, he treats the object itself, in the brass model, as if it were the piston of an engine: the tapering is as delicate, the polish is as high, as if it were to be fitted into the most intricate piece of machinery, in which so much as a few specks of dust would interfere with its perfect action: looking at the bird, one thinks of the shell of a torpedo. As for the bird itself, it is no longer any particular bird, but a generic bird in its most birdlike aspect, the function of flight. So, too, with his metallic or marble fish, looking like experimental forms developed in an aviation laboratory, floating on the flawless surface of a mirror. Here is the equivalent in art of the mechanical world that lies about us on every hand: with this further perfection of the symbol, that in the highly polished metallic forms the world as a whole and the spectator himself, are likewise mirrored: so that the old separation between subject and object is now figuratively closed. The obtuse United States customs officer who wished to classify Brancusi's sculpture as machinery or plumbing was in fact paying it a compliment. In Brancusi's sculpture the idea of the machine is objectified and assimilated in equivalent works of art.

In this perception of the machine as a source of art, the new painters and sculptors clarified the whole issue and delivered art from the romantic prejudice against the machine as necessarily hostile to the world of feeling. At the same time, they began to interpret intuitively the new conceptions of time and space that distinguish the present age from the Renascence. The course of this development can perhaps be followed best in the photograph and the motion picture: the specific arts of the machine.

4: Photography as Means and Symbol

The history of the camera, and of its product, the photograph, illustrates the typical dilemmas that have arisen in the development of the machine process and its application to objects of esthetic value. Both the special feats of the machine and its possible perversions are equally manifest.

At first, the limitations of the camera were a safeguard to its intelligent use. The photographer, still occupied with difficult photo-chemical and optical problems, did not attempt to extract from the photograph any other values than those rendered immediately by the technique itself; and as a result, the grave portraiture of some of the early photographers, particularly that of David Octavius Hill of Edinburgh, reached a high pitch of excellence: indeed it has not often been surpassed by any of the later work. As the technical problems were solved one by one, through the use of better lenses, more sensitive emulsions, new textures of paper to replace the shiny surface of the daguerreotype, the photographer became more conscious of the esthetic arrangements of the subjects before him: instead of carrying the esthetic of the light-picture further, he returned timidly to the canons of painting, and endeavored to make his pictures fit certain preconceptions of beauty as achieved by the classical painters. Far from glorying in minute and tangled representation of life, as the mechanical eye confronts it, the photographer from the eighties onward sought by means of soft lenses a foggy impressionism, or by care of arrangement and theatrical lighting he attempted to imitate the postures and sometimes the costumes of Holbein and Gainsborough. Some experimenters even went so far as to imitate in the photographic print the smudgy effect of charcoal or the crisp lines of the etching. This relapse from clean mechanical processes to an artful imitativeness worked ruin in photography for a full generation: it was like that relapse in the technique of furniture making which used modern machinery to imitate the dead forms of antique handicraft. In back of it was the failure to understand the intrinsic esthetic importance of the new mechanical device in terms of its own peculiar possibilities.

Every photograph, no matter how painstaking the observation of the photographer or how long the actual exposure, is essentially a snapshot: it is an attempt to penetrate and capture the unique esthetic moment that singles itself out of the thousand of chance compositions, uncrystallized and insignificant, that occur in the course of a day. The photographer cannot rearrange his material on his own terms. He must take the world as he finds it: at most his rearrangement is limited to a change in position or an alteration of the direction and intensity of the light or in the length of the focus. He must respect and understand sunlight, atmosphere, the time of day, the season of the year, the capabilities of the machine, the processes of chemical development; for the mechanical device does not function automatically, and the results depend upon the exact correlation of the esthetic moment itself with the appropriate physical means. But whereas an underlying technique conditions both painting and photography—for the painter, too, must respect the chemical composition of his colors and the physical conditions which will give them permanence and visibility—photography differs from the other graphic arts in that the process is determined at every state by the external conditions that present themselves: his inner impulse, instead of spreading itself in subjective fantasy, must always be in key with outer circumstances. As for the various kinds of *montage* photography, they are in reality not photography at all but a kind of painting, in which the photograph is used—as patches of textiles are used in crazy-quilts—to form a mosaic. Whatever value the montage may have derives from the painting rather than the camera.

Rare though painting of the first order is, photography of the first rank is perhaps even rarer. The gamut of emotion and significance represented in photography by the work of Alfred Stieglitz in America is one that the photographer rarely spans. Half the merit of Stieglitz' work is due to his rigorous respect for the limitations of the machine and to the subtlety with which he effects the combination of image and paper. He plays no tricks, he has no affectations, not even the affectation of being hard-boiled, for life and the object have their soft moments and their tender aspects. The mission of the photograph is to clarify the object. This objectification, this clarification, are important developments in the mind itself: it is perhaps the prime psychological fact that emerges with our rational assimilation of the machine. To see as they are, as if for the first time, a boatload of immigrants, a tree in Madison Square Park, a woman's breast, a cloud lowering over a black mountain—that requires patience and understanding. Ordinarily we skip over and schematize these objects, relate them to some practical need, or subordinate them to some immediate wish: photography gives us the ability to recognize them in the independent form created by light and shade and shadow. Good photography, then, is one of the best educations toward a rounded sense of reality. Restoring to the eye, otherwise so preoccupied with the abstractions of print, the stimulus of things roundly seen as things, shapes, colors, textures, demanding for its enjoyment a previous experience of light and shade, this machine process in itself counteracts some of the worst defects of our mechanical environment. It is the hopeful antithesis to an emasculated and segregated esthetic sensibility, the cult of pure form, which endeavors to hide away from the world that ultimately gives shape and significance to its remotest symbols.

If photography has become popular again in our own day, after its first great but somewhat sentimental outburst in the eighties, it is perhaps because, like an invalid returning to health, we are finding a new delight in being, seeing, touching, feeling; because in a rural or a neotechnic environment the sunlight and pure air that make it possible are present; because, too, we have at least learned Whitman's lesson and behold with a new respect the miracle of our finger joints or the reality of a blade of grass: photography is not least effective when it is dealing with such ultimate simplicities. To disdain photography because it cannot achieve what El Greco or Rembrandt or Tintoretto achieved is like dismissing science because its view of the world is not comparable to the visions of Plotinus or the mythologies of Hinduism. Its virtue lies precisely in the fact that it has conquered another and quite different department of reality. For photography, finally, gives the effect of permanence to the transient and the ephemeral: photography—and perhaps photography alone—is capable of coping with and adequately presenting the complicated, inter-related aspects of our modern environment. As histories of the human comedy of our times, the photographs of Atget in Paris and of Stieglitz in New York are unique both as drama and as document: not merely do they convey to us the very shape and touch of this environment, but by the angle of vision and the moment of observation throw an oblique light upon our inner lives, our hopes, our values, our humours. And this art, of all our arts, is perhaps the most widely used and the most fully enjoyed: the amateur, the specialist, the news-photographer, and the common man have all participated in this eye-opening experience, and in this discovery of that esthetic moment which is the common property of all experience, at all its various levels from ungoverned dream to brute action and rational idea.

What has been said of the photograph applies even more, perhaps, to the motion picture. In its first exploitation the motion picture emphasized its unique quality: the possibility of abstracting and reproducing objects in motion: the simple races and chases of the early pictures pointed the art in the right direction. But in its subsequent commercial development it was degraded a little by the attempt to make it the vehicle of a short-story or a novel or a drama: a mere imitation in vision of entirely different arts. So one must distinguish between the motion picture as an indifferent reproductive device, less satisfactory in most ways than direct production on the stage, and the motion picture as an art in its own right. The great achievements of the motion picture have been in the presentation of history or natural history, the sequences of actuality, or in their interpretation of the inner realm of fantasy, as in the pure comedies of Charlie Chaplin and René Clair and Walt Disney. Unlike the photograph, the extremes of subjectivism and of factualism meet in the motion picture. Nanook of the North, Chang, the S.S. Potemkin—these pictures got their dramatic effect through their interpretation of an immediate experience and through a heightened delight in actuality. Their exoticism was entirely accidental: an equally good eye would abstract the same order of significant events from the day's routine of a subway guard or a factory-hand: indeed, the most consistently interesting pictures have been those of the newsreel—despite the insufferable banality of the announcers who too often accompany them.

Not plot in the old dramatic sense, but historic and geographic sequences is the key to the arrangement of these new kinetic compositions: the passage of objects, organisms, dream images through time and space. It is an unfortunate social accident—as has happened in so many departments of technics—that this art should have been grossly diverted from its proper function by the commercial necessity for creating sentimental shows for an emotionally empty metropolitanized population, living vicariously on the kisses and cocktails and crimes and orgies and murders of their shadow-idols. For the motion picture symbolizes and expresses, better than do any of the traditional arts, our modern world picture and the essential conceptions of time and space which are already part of the unformulated experience of millions of people, to whom Einstein or Bohr or Bergson or Alexander are scarcely even names.

In Gothic painting one may recall time and space were successive and unrelated: the immediate and the eternal, the near and the far, were confused: the faithful time ordering of the medieval chroniclers is marred by the jumble of events presented and by the impossibility of distinguishing hearsay from observation and fact from conjecture. In the Renascence space and time were co-ordinated within a single system: but the axis of these events remained fixed, so to say, within a single frame established at a set distance from the observer, whose existence with reference to the system was innocently taken for granted. Today, in the motion picture, which symbolizes our actual perceptions and feelings, time and space are not merely co-ordinated on their own axis, but in relation to an observer who himself, by his position, partly determines the picture, and who is no longer fixed but is likewise capable of motion. The moving picture, with its close-ups and its synoptic views, with its shifting events and its ever-present camera eye, with its spatial forms always shown through time, with its capacity for representing objects that interpenetrate, and for placing distant environments in immediate juxtaposition—as happens in instantaneous communication—with its ability, finally, to represent subjective elements, distortions, hallucinations, it is today the only art that can represent with any degree of concreteness the emergent world-view that differentiates our culture from every preceding one.

Even with weak and trivial subjects, the art focusses interests and captures values that the traditional arts leave untouched. Music alone heretofore has represented movement through time: but the motion picture synthesizes movement through both time and space, and in the very fact that it can co-ordinate visual images with sound and release both of these elements from the boundaries of apparent space and a fixed location, it contributes something to our picture of the world not given completely in direct experience. Utilizing our daily experience of motion in the railroad train and the motor car, the motion picture re-creates in symbolic form a world that is otherwise beyond our direct perception or grasp. Without any conscious notion of its destination, the motion picture presents us with a world of interpenetrating, counter-influencing organisms: and it enables us to think about that world with a greater degree of concreteness. This is no small triumph in cultural assimilation. Though it has been so stupidly misused, the motion picture nevertheless announces itself as a major art of the neotechnic phase. Through the machine, we have new possibilities of understanding the world we have helped to create.

But in the arts, it is plain that the machine is an instrument with manifold and conflicting possibilities. It may be used as a passive substitute for experience; it may be used to counterfeit older forms of art; it may also be used, in its own right, to concentrate and intensify and express new forms of experience. As substitutes for primary experience, the machine is worthless: indeed it is actually debilitating. Just as the microscope is useless unless the eye itself is keen, so all our mechanical apparatus in the arts depends for its success upon the due cultivation of the organic, physiological, and spiritual aptitudes that lie behind its use. The machine cannot be used as a shortcut to escape the necessity for organic experience. Mr. Waldo Frank has put the matter well: "Art," he says, "cannot become a language, hence an experience, unless it is practiced. To the man who plays, a mechanical reproduction of music may mean much, since he already has the experience to assimilate. But where reproduction becomes the norm, the few music makers will grow more isolate and sterile, and the ability to experience music will disappear. The same is true with the cinema, dance, and even sport."

Whereas in industry the machine may properly replace the human being when he has been reduced to an automaton, in the arts the machine can only extend and deepen man's original functions and intuitions. In so far as the phonograph and the radio do away with the impulse to sing, in so far as the camera does away with the impulse to see, in so far as the automobile does away with the impulse to walk, the machine leads to a lapse of function which is but one step away from paralysis. But in the application of mechanical instruments to the arts it is not the machine itself that we must fear. The chief danger lies in the failure to integrate the arts themselves with the totality of our life-experience: the perverse triumph of the machine follows automatically from the abdication of the spirit. Consciously to assimilate the machine is one means of reducing its omnipotence. We cannot, as Karl Buecher wisely said, "give up the hope that it will be possible to unite technics and art in a higher rhythmical unity, which will restore to the spirit the fortunate serenity and to the body the harmonious cultivation that manifest themselves at their best among primitive peoples." The machine has not destroyed that promise. On the contrary, through the more conscious cultivation of the machine arts and through greater selectivity in their use, one sees the pledge of its wider fulfillment throughout civilization. For at the bottom of that cultivation there must be the direct and immediate experience of living itself: we must directly see, feel, touch, manipulate, sing, dance, communicate before we can extract from the machine any further sustenance for life. If we are empty to begin with, the machine will only leave us emptier; if we are passive and powerless to begin with, the machine will only leave us more feeble.

5: The Growth of Functionalism

But modern technics, even apart from the special arts that it fostered, had a cultural contribution to make in its own right. Just as science underlined the respect for fact, so technics emphasized the importance of function: in this domain, as Emerson pointed out, the beautiful rests on the foundations of the necessary. The nature of this contribution can best be shown, perhaps, by describing the way in which the problem of machine design was first faced, then evaded, and finally solved.

One of the first products of the machine was the machine itself. As in the organization of the first factories the narrowly practical considerations were uppermost, and all the other needs of the personality were firmly shoved to one side. The machine was a direct expression of its own functions: the first cannon, the first crossbows, the first steam engines were all nakedly built for action. But once the primary problems of organization and operation had been solved, the human factor, which had been left out of the picture, needed somehow to be re-incorporated. The only precedent for this fuller integration of form came naturally from handicraft: hence over the incomplete, only partly realized forms of the early cannon, the early bridges, the early machines, a meretricious touch of decoration was added: a mere relic of the happy, semi-magical fantasies that painting and carving had once added to every handicraft object. Because perhaps the energies of the eotechnic period were so completely engrossed in the technical problems, it was, from the standpoint of design, amazingly clean and direct: ornament flourished in the utilities of life, flourished often perversely and extravagantly, but one looks for it in vain among the machines pictured by Agricola or Besson or the Italian engineers: they are as direct and factual as was architecture from the tenth to the thirteenth century.

The worst sinners—that is the most obvious sentimentalists—were the engineers of the paleotechnic period. In the act of recklessly deflowering the environment at large, they sought to expiate their failures by adding a few sprigs or posies to the new engines they were creating: they embellished their steam engines with Doric columns or partly concealed them behind Gothic tracery: they decorated the frames of their presses and their automatic machines with cast-iron arabesque, they punched ornamental holes in the iron framework of their new structures, from the trusses of the old wing of the Metropolitan Museum to the base of the Eiffel tower in Paris. Everywhere similar habits prevailed: the homage of hypocrisy to art. One notes identical efforts on the original steam radiators, in the floral decorations that once graced typewriters, in the nondescript ornament that still lingers quaintly on shotguns and sewing machines, even if it has at length disappeared from cash registers and Pullman cars—as long before, in the first uncertainties of the new technics, the same division had appeared in armor and in crossbows.

The second stage in machine design was a compromise. The object was divided into two parts. One of them was to be precisely designed for mechanical efficiency. The other was to be designed for looks. While the utilitarian claimed the working parts of the structure the esthete was, so to speak, permitted slightly to modify the surfaces with his unimportant patterns, his plutonic flowers, his aimless filigree, provided he did not seriously weaken the structure or condemn the function to inefficiency. Mechanically utilizing the machine, this type of design shamefully attempted to conceal the origins that were still felt as low and mean. The engineer had the uneasiness of a parvenu, and the same impulse to imitate the most archaic patterns of his betters.

Naturally the next stage was soon reached: the utilitarian and the esthete withdrew again to their respective fields. The esthete, insisting with justice that the structure was integral with the decoration and that art was something more fundamental than the icing the pastrycook put on the cake, sought to make the old decoration real by altering the nature of the structure. Taking his place as workman, he began to revive the purely handicraft methods of the weaver, the cabinet maker, the printer, arts that had survived for the most part only in the more backward parts of the world, untouched by the tourist and the commercial traveller. The old workshops and ateliers were languishing and dying out in the nineteenth century, especially in progressive England and in America, when new ones, like those devoted to glass under William de Morgan in England, and John La Farge in America, and Lalique in France, or to a miscellany of handicrafts, such as that of William Morris in England, sprang into existence, to prove by their example that the arts of the past could survive. The industrial manufacturer, isolated from this movement yet affected by it, contemptuous but half-convinced, made an effort to retrieve his position by attempting to copy mechanically the dead forms of art he found in the museum. So far from gaining from the handicrafts movement by this procedure he lost what little virtue his untutored designs possessed, issuing as they sometimes did out of an intimate knowledge of the processes and the materials.

The weakness of the original handicrafts movement was that it assumed that the only important change in industry had been the intrusion of the soulless machine. Whereas the fact was that everything had changed, and all the shapes and patterns employed by technics were therefore bound to change, too. The world men carried in their heads, their idolum, was entirely different from that which set the medieval mason to carving the history of creation or the lives of the saints above the portals of the cathedral, or a jolly image of some sort above his own doorway. An art based like handicraft upon a certain stratification of the classes and the social differentiation of the arts could not survive in a world where men had seen the French Revolution and had been promised some rough share of equality. Modern handicraft, which sought to rescue the worker from the slavery of shoddy machine production, merely enabled the well-to-do to enjoy new objects that were as completely divorced from the dominant social milieu as the palaces and monasteries that the antiquarian art dealer and collector had begun to loot. The *educational aim* of the arts and crafts movement was admirable; and, in so far as it gave courage and understanding to the amateur, it was a success. If this movement did not add a sufficient amount of good handicraft it at least took away a great deal of false art. William Morris's dictum, that one should not possess anything one did not believe to be beautiful or know to be useful was, in the shallow showy bourgeois world he addressed, a revolutionary dictum.

But the social outcome of the arts and crafts movement was not commensurate with the needs of the new situation; as Mr. Frank Lloyd Wright pointed out in his memorable speech at Hull House in 1908, the machine itself was as much an instrument of art, in the hands of an artist, as were the simple tools and utensils. To erect a social barrier between machines and tools was really to accept the false notion of the new industrialist who, bent on exploiting the machine, which they owned, and jealous of the tool, which might still be owned by the independent worker, bestowed on the machine an exclusive sanctity and grace it did not merit. Lacking the courage to use the machine as an instrument of creative purpose, and being unable to attune themselves to new objectives and new standards, the esthetes were logically compelled to restore a medieval ideology in order to provide a social backing for their anti-machine bias. In a word, the arts and crafts movement did not grasp the fact that the new technics, by expanding the rôle of the machine, had altered the entire relation of handwork to production, and that the exact processes of the machine were not necessarily hostile to handicraft and fine workmanship. In its modern form handicraft could no longer serve as in the past when it had worked under the form of an intensive caste-specialization. To survive, handicraft would have to adapt itself to the amateur, and it was bound to call into existence, even in pure handwork, those forms of economy and simplicity which the machine was claiming for its own, and to which it was adapting mind and hand and eye. In this process of re-integration certain "eternal" forms would be recovered: there are handicraft forms dating back to a distant past which so completely fulfill their functions that no amount of further calculation or experiment will alter them for the better. These type-forms appear and reappear from civilization to civilization; and if they had not been discovered by handicraft, the machine would have had to invent them.

The new handicraft was in fact to receive presently a powerful lesson from the machine. For the forms created by the machine, when they no longer sought to imitate old superficial patterns of handwork, were closer to those that could be produced by the amateur than were, for example, the intricacies of special joints, fine inlays, matched woods, beads and carvings, complicated forms of metallic ornament, the boast of handicraft in the past. While in the factory the machine was often reduced to producing fake handicraft, in the workshop of the amateur the reverse process could take place with a real gain: he was liberated by the very simplicities of good machine forms. Machine technique as a means to achieving a simplified and purified form relieved the amateur from the need of respecting and imitating the perversely complicated patterns of the past—patterns whose complications were partly the result of conspicuous waste, partly the outcome of technical virtuosity, and partly the result of a different state of feeling. But before handicraft could thus be restored as an admirable form of play and an efficacious relief from

a physically untutored life, it was necessary to dispose of the machine itself as a social and esthetic instrument. So the major contribution to art was made, after all, by the industrialist who remained
on the job and saw it through.

With the third stage in machine design an alteration takes place.
The imagination is not applied to the mechanical object after the
practical design has been completed: it is infused into it at every
stage in development. The mind works through the medium of the
machine directly, respects the conditions imposed upon it, and—not
content with a crude quantitative approximation—seeks out a more
positive esthetic fulfillment. This must not be confused with the
dogma, so often current, that any mechanical contraption that works
necessarily is esthetically interesting. The source of this fallacy is
plain. In many cases, indeed, our eyes have been trained to recognize beauty in nature, and with certain kinds of animals and birds
we have an especial sympathy. When an airplane becomes like a
gull it has the advantage of this long association and we properly
couple the beauty with the mechanical adequacy, since the poise and
swoop of a gull's flight casts in addition a reflective beauty on its
animal structure. Having no such association with a milkweed seed,
we do not feel the same beauty in the autogyro, which is kept aloft
by a similar principle. While genuine beauty in a thing of use must
always be joined to mechanical adequacy and therefore involves
a certain amount of intellectual recognition and appraisal, the relation is not a simple one: it points to a common source rather than an
identity.

In the conception of a machine or of a product of the machine
there is a point where one may leave off for parsimonious reasons
without having reached esthetic perfection: at this point perhaps
every mechanical factor is accounted for, and the sense of incom-
pleteness is due to the failure to recognize the claims of the human
agent. Esthetics carries with it the implication of alternatives between a number of mechanical solutions of equal validity: and
unless this awareness is present at every stage of the process, in
smaller matters of finish, fineness, trimness, it is not likely to come
out with any success in the final stage of design. Form follows func-

tion, underlining it, crystallizing it, clarifying it, making it real to the eye. Makeshifts and approximations express themselves in incomplete forms: forms like the absurdly cumbrous and ill-adjusted telephone apparatus of the past, like the old-fashioned airplane, full of struts, wires, extra supports, all testifying to an anxiety to cover innumerable unknown or uncertain factors; forms like the old automobile in which part after part had been added to the effective mechanism without having been absorbed into the body of the design as a whole; forms like our oversized steel-work which were due to our carelessness in using cheap materials and our desire to avoid the extra expense of calculating them finely and expending the necessary labor to work them up. The impulse that creates a complete mechanical object is akin to that which creates an esthetically finished object; and the fusion of the two at every stage in the process will necessarily be effected by the environment at large: who can gauge how much the slatternliness and disorder of the paleotechnic environment undermined good design, or how much the order and beauty of our neotechnic plants—like that of the Van Nelle factory in Rotterdam—will eventually aid it? Esthetic interests can not suddenly be introduced from without: they must be constantly operative, constantly visible.

Expression through the machine implies the recognition of relatively new esthetic terms: precision, calculation, flawlessness, simplicity, economy. Feeling attaches itself in these new forms to different qualities than those that made handicraft so entertaining. Success here consists in the elimination of the non-essential, rather than, as in handicraft decoration, in the willing production of superfluity, contributed by the worker out of his own delight in the work. The elegance of a mathematical equation, the inevitability of a series of physical inter-relations, the naked quality of the material itself, the tight logic of the whole—these are the ingredients that go into the design of machines: and they go equally into products that have been properly designed for machine production. In handicraft it is the worker who is represented: in machine design it is the work. In handicraft, the personal touch is emphasized, and the imprint of the worker and his tool are both inevitable: in machine work the impersonal prevails, and if the worker leaves any tell-tale evidence of his part in the operation, it is a defect or a flaw. Hence the burden of machine design is in the making of the original pattern: it is here that trials are made, that errors are discovered and buried, that the creative process as a whole is concentrated. Once the master-pattern is set, the rest is routine: beyond the designing room and the laboratory there is—for goods produced on a serial basis for a mass market—no opportunity for choice and personal achievement. Hence apart from those commodities that can be produced automatically, the effort of sound industrial production must be to increase the province of the designing room and the laboratory, reducing the scale of the production, and making possible an easier passage back and forth between the designing and the operative sections of the plant.

Who discovered these new canons of machine design? Many an engineer and many a machine worker must have mutely sensed them and reached toward them: indeed, one sees the beginning of them in very early mechanical instruments. But only after centuries of more or less blind and unformulated effort were these canons finally demonstrated with a certain degree of completeness in the work of the great engineers toward the end of the nineteenth century—particularly the Roeblings in America and Eiffel in France—and formulated after that by theoreticians like Riedler and Meyer in Germany. The popularization of the new esthetic awaited, as I have pointed out, the post-impressionist painters. They contributed by breaking away from the values of purely associative art and by abolishing an undue concern for natural objects as the basis of the painter's interest: if on one side this led to completer subjectivism, on the other it tended toward a recognition of the machine as both form and symbol. In the same direction Marcel Duchamp, for example, who was one of the leaders of this movement, made a collection of cheap, ready-made articles, produced by the machine, and called attention to their esthetic soundness and sufficiency. In many cases, the finest designs had been achieved before any conscious recognition of the esthetic had taken place. With the coming of a commercialized designer, seeking to add "art" to a product which *was* art, the design has more often than not been trifled with and spoiled. The studious botching of the kodak, the bathroom fixture, and the steam radiator under such stylicizing is a current commonplace.

The key to this fresh appreciation of the machine as a source of new esthetic forms has come through a formulation of its chief esthetic principle: the principle of economy. This principle is of course not unknown in other phases of art: but the point is that in mechanical forms it is at all times a controlling one, and it has for its aid the more exact calculations and measurements that are now possible. The aim of sound design is to remove from the object, be it an automobile or a set of china or a room, every detail, every moulding, every variation of the surface, every extra part except that which conduces to its effective functioning. Toward the working out of this principle, our mechanical habits and our unconscious impulses have been tending steadily. In departments where esthetic choices are not consciously uppermost our taste has often been excellent and sure. Le Corbusier has been very ingenious in picking out manifold objects, buried from observation by their very ubiquity, in which this mechanical excellence of form has manifested itself without pretence or fumbling. Take the smoking pipe: it is no longer carved to look like a human head nor does it bear, except among college students, any heraldic emblems: it has become exquisitely anonymous, being nothing more than an apparatus for supplying drafts of smoke to the human mouth from a slow-burning mass of vegetation. Take the ordinary drinking glass in a cheap restaurant: it is no longer cut or cast or engraved with special designs: at most it may have a slight bulge near the top to keep one glass from sticking to another in stacking: it is as clean, as functional, as a high tension insulator. Or take the present watch and its case and compare it with the forms that handicraft ingenuity and taste and association created in the sixteenth or seventeenth centuries. In all the commoner objects of our environment the machine canons are instinctively accepted: even the most sentimental manufacturer of motor cars has not been tempted to paint his coach work to resemble a sedan chair in the style of Watteau, although he may live in a house in which the furniture and decoration are treated in that perverse fashion.

This stripping down to essentials has gone on in every department of machine work and has touched every aspect of life. It is a first step toward that completer integration of the machine with human needs and desires which is the mark of the neotechnic phase, and will be even more the mark of the biotechnic period, already visible over the edge of the horizon. As in the social transition from the paleotechnic to the neotechnic order, the chief obstacle to the fuller development of the machine lies in the association of taste and fashion with waste and commercial profiteering. For the rational development of genuine technical standards, based on function and performance, can come about only by a wholesale devaluation of the scheme of bourgeois civilization upon which our present system of production is based.

Capitalism, which along with war played such a stimulating part in the development of technics, now remains with war the chief obstacle toward its further improvement. The reason should be plain. The machine devaluates rarity: instead of producing a single unique object, it is capable of producing a million others just as good as the master model from which the rest are made. The machine devaluates age: for age is another token of rarity, and the machine, by placing its emphasis upon fitness and adaptation, prides itself on the brand-new rather than on the antique: instead of feeling comfortably authentic in the midst of rust, dust, cobwebs, shaky parts, it prides itself on the opposite qualities—slickness, smoothness, gloss, cleanness. The machine devaluates archaic taste: for taste in the bourgeois sense is merely another name for pecuniary reputability, and against that standard the machine sets up the standards of function and fitness. The newest, the cheapest, the commonest objects may, from the standpoint of pure esthetics, be immensely superior to the rarest, the most expensive, and the most antique. To say all this is merely to emphasize that the modern technics, by its own essential nature, imposes a great purification of esthetics: that is, it strips off from the object all the barnacles of association, all the sentimental and pecuniary values which have nothing whatever to do with esthetic form, and it focusses attention upon the object itself.

The social devaluation of caste, enforced by the proper use and appreciation of the machine, is as important as the stripping down of essential forms in the process itself. One of the happiest signs of this during the last decade was the use of cheap and common materials in jewelry, first introduced, I believe, by Lalique: for this implied a recognition of the fact that an esthetically appropriate form, even in the adornment of the body, has nothing to do with rarity or expense, but is a matter of color, shape, line, texture, fitness, symbol. The use of cheap cottons in dress by Chanel and her imitators, which was another post-war phenomenon, was an equally happy recognition of the essential values in our new economy: it at last put our civilization, if only momentarily, on the level of those primitive cultures which gladly bartered their furs and ivory for the white man's colored glass beads, by the adroit use of which the savage artist often proved to any disinterested observer that they— contrary to the white man's fatuous conceit—had gotten the better of the bargain. Because of the fact that woman's dress has a peculiarly compensatory rôle to play in our megalopolitan society, so that it more readily indicates what is absent than calls attention to what is present in it, the victory for genuine esthetics could only be a temporary one. But these forms of dress and jewelry pointed to the goal of machine production: the goal at which each object would be valued in terms of its direct mechanical and vital and social function, apart from its pecuniary status, the snobberies of caste, or the dead sentiments of historical emulation.

This warfare between a sound machine esthetic and what Veblen has called the "requirements of pecuniary reputability" has still another side. Our modern technology has, in its inner organization, produced a collective economy and its typical products are collective products. Whatever the politics of a country may be, the machine is a communist: hence the deep contradictions and conflicts that have kept on developing in machine industry since the end of the eighteenth century. At every stage in technics, the work represents a collaboration of innumerable workers, themselves utilizing a large and ramifying technological heritage: the most ingenious inventor, the most brilliant individual scientist, the most skilled designer contributes but a moiety to the final result. And the product itself necessarily bears the same impersonal imprint: it either functions or it does not function on quite impersonal lines. There can be no qualitative difference between a poor man's electric bulb of a given candlepower and a rich man's, to indicate their differing pecuniary status in society, although there was an enormous difference between the rush or stinking tallow of the peasant and the wax candles or sperm oil used by the upper classes before the coming of gas and electricity.

In so far as pecuniary differences are permitted to count in the machine economy, they can alter only the scale of things—not, in terms of present production, the kind. What applies to electric light bulbs applies to automobiles: what applies there applies equally to every manner of apparatus or utility. The frantic attempts that have been made in America by advertising agencies and "designers" to stylicize machine-made objects have been, for the most part, attempts to pervert the machine process in the interests of caste and pecuniary distinction. In money-ridden societies, where men play with poker chips instead of with economic and esthetic realities, every attempt is made to disguise the fact that the machine has achieved potentially a new collective economy, in which the possession of goods is a meaningless distinction, since the machine can produce all our essential goods in unparalleled qualities, falling on the just and the unjust, the foolish and the wise, like the rain itself.

The conclusion is obvious: we cannot intelligently accept the practical benefits of the machine without accepting its moral imperatives and its esthetic forms. Otherwise both ourselves and our society will be the victims of a shattering disunity, and one set of purposes, that which created the order of the machine, will be constantly at war with trivial and inferior personal impulses bent on working out in covert ways our psychological weaknesses. Lacking on the whole this rational acceptance, we have lost a good part of the practical benefits of the machine and have achieved esthetic expression only in a spotty, indecisive way. The real social distinction of modern technics, however, is that it tends to eliminate social distinctions. Its immediate goal is effective work. Its means are standardization: the emphasis of the generic and the typical: in short, conspicuous economy. Its ultimate aim is leisure—that is, the release of other organic capacities.

The powerful esthetic side of this social process has been obscured by speciously pragmatic and pecuniary interests that have inserted themselves into our technology and have imposed themselves upon its legitimate aims. But in spite of this deflection of effort, we have at last begun to realize these new values, these new forms, these new modes of expression. Here is a new environment—man's extension of nature in terms discovered by the close observation and analysis and abstraction of nature. The elements of this environment are hard and crisp and clear: the steel bridge, the concrete road, the turbine and the alternator, the glass wall. Behind the façade are rows and rows of machines, weaving cotton, transporting coal, assembling food, printing books, machines with steel fingers and lean muscular arms, with perfect reflexes, sometimes even with electric eyes. Alongside them are the new utilities—the coke oven, the transformer, the dye vats—chemically cooperating with these mechanical processes, assembling new qualities in chemical compounds and materials. Every effective part in this whole environment represents an effort of the collective mind to widen the province of order and control and provision. And here, finally, the perfected forms begin to hold human interest even apart from their practical performances: they tend to produce that inner composure and equilibrium, that sense of balance between the inner impulse and the outer environment, which is one of the marks of a work of art. The machines, even when they are not works of art, underlie our art—that is, our organized perceptions and feelings—in the way that Nature underlies them, extending the basis upon which we operate and confirming our own impulse to order. The economic: the objective: the collective: and finally the integration of these principles in a new conception of the organic—these are the marks, already discernible, of our assimilation of the machine not merely as an instrument of practical action but as a valuable mode of life.

6: The Simplification of the Environment

As a practical instrument, the machine has enormously complicated the environment. When one compares the shell of an eighteenth
century house with the tangle of water-pipes, gas-pipes, electric wires,
sewers, aerials, ventilators, heating and cooling systems that compose
a modern house, or when one compares the cobblestones of the old-
fashioned street, set directly on the earth, with the cave of cables,
pipes, and subway systems that run under the asphalt, one has no
doubt about the mechanical intricacy of modern existence.

But precisely because there are so many physical organs, and
because so many parts of our environment compete constantly for
our attention, we need to guard ourselves against the fatigue of dealing with too many objects or being stimulated unnecessarily by their
presence, as we perform the numerous offices they impose. Hence a
simplification of the externals of the mechanical world is almost a
prerequisite for dealing with its internal complications. To reduce
the constant succession of stimuli, the environment itself must be
made as neutral as possible. This, again, is partly in opposition to
the principle of many handicraft arts, where the effort is to hold the
eye, to give the mind something to play with, to claim a special
attention for itself. So that if the canon of economy and the respect
for function were not rooted in modern technics, it would have to be
derived from our psychological reaction to the machine: only by
esthetically observing these principles can the chaos of stimuli be
reduced to the point of effective assimilation.

Without standardization, without repetition, without the neutral-
izing effect of habit, our mechanical environment might well, by
reason of its tempo and its continuous impact, be too formidable: in
departments which have not been sufficiently simplified it exceeds
the limit of toleration. The machine has thus, in its esthetic manifestations, something of the same effect that a conventional code of
manners has in social intercourse: it removes the strain of contact
and adjustment. The standardization of manners is a psychological
shock-absorber: it permits intercourse between persons and groups
to take place without the preliminary exploration and understanding

that are requisite for an ultimate adjustment. In the province of esthetics, this simplification has still a further use: it gives small deviations and variations from the prevalent norm the psychological refreshment that would go only with much larger changes under a condition where variation was the expected mode and standardization was the exception. Mr. A. N. Whitehead has pointed out that one of our chief literary sins is in thinking of past and future in terms of a thousand years forward and backward, when really to experience the organic nature of past and future one should think of time in the order of a second, or a fraction of a second. One can make a similar remark about our esthetic perceptions: those who complain about the standardization of the machine are used to thinking of variations in terms of gross changes in pattern and structure, such as those that take place between totally different cultures or generations; whereas one of the signs of a rational enjoyment of the machine and the machine-made environment is to be concerned with much smaller differences and to react sensitively to them.

To feel the difference between two elemental types of window, with a slightly different ratio in the division of lights, rather than to feel it only when one of them is in a steel frame and the other is surmounted by a broken pediment, is the mark of a fine esthetic consciousness in our emerging culture. Good craftsmen have always had some of this finer sense of form: but it was confused by the snobbish taste and arbitrary literary standards of form that came into court life during the Renascence. As the various parts of our environment become more standardized, the senses must in turn become more acute, more refined: a hair's breadth, a speck of dirt, a faint wave in the surface will distress us as much as the pea hurt Hans Andersen's princess, and similarly pleasure will derive from delicacies of adaptation to which most of us are now indifferent. Standardization, which economizes our attention when our minds have other work to do, serves as the substratum in those departments where we deliberately seek esthetic satisfaction.

In creating the machine, we have set before ourselves a positively inhuman standard of perfection. No matter what the occasion, the criterion of successful mechanical form is that it should look *as if* no human hand had touched it. In that effort, in that boast, in that achievement the human hand shows itself, perhaps, in its most cunning manifestation. And yet ultimately it is to the human organism that we must return to achieve the final touch of perfection: the finest reproduction still lacks something that the original picture possessed: the finest porcelain produced with the aid of every mechanical accessory lacks the perfection of the great Chinese potters: the finest mechanical printing lacks that complete union of black and white that hand-printing produces with its slower method and its dampened paper. Very frequently, in machine work, the best structure is forfeited to the mere conveniences of production: given equally high standards of performance, the machine can often no more than hold its own in competition with the hand product. The pinnacles of handicraft art set a standard that the machine must constantly hold before it; but against this one must recognize that in a hundred departments examples of supreme skill and refinement have, thanks to the machine, become a commonplace. And at all levels, this esthetic refinement spreads out into life: it appears in surgery and dentistry as well as in the design of houses and bridges and high-tension power lines. The direct effect of these techniques upon the designers, workers, and manipulators cannot be over-estimated. Whatever the tags, archaicisms, verbalisms, emotional and intellectual mischiefs of our regnant system of education, the machine itself as a constant educator cannot be neglected. If during the paleotechnic period the machine accentuated the brutality of the mine, in the neotechnic phase it promises, if we use it intelligently, to restore the delicacy and sensitivity of the organism.

7: The Objective Personality

Granting these new instruments, this new environment, these new perceptions and sensations and standards, this new daily routine, these new esthetic responses—what sort of man comes out of modern technics? Le Play once asked his auditors what was the most important thing that came out of the mine; and after one had guessed coal and another iron and another gold, he answered: No, the most important thing that comes out of the mine is the miner. That is true for every occupation. And today every type of work has been affected by the machine.

I have already discussed, in terms of their limitations and renunciations, the type of man that influenced modern mechanization: the monk, the soldier, the miner, the financier. But the fuller experience of the machine does not necessarily tend to produce a repetition of these original patterns—although there is plenty of evidence to show that the soldier and the financier occupy a larger position in our world today than at perhaps any other time in the past. In the act of expressing themselves with the aid of the machine, the capacities of these original types have been modified and their character altered; moreover, what was once the innovation of a daring race of pioneers has now become the settled routine of a vast mass of people who have taken over the habits without having shared any of the original enthusiasm, and many of the latter still perhaps have no special bent toward the machine. It is difficult to analyze out such a pervasive influence as this: no single cause is at work, no single reaction can be attributed solely to the machine. And we who live in this medium; and who have been formed by it, who constantly breathe it and adapt ourselves to it, cannot possibly measure the deflection caused by the medium, still less estimate the drift of the machine, and all it carries with it, from other norms. The only partial corrective is to examine a more primitive environment, as Mr. Stuart Chase attempted to do; but even here one cannot correct for the way in which our very questions and our scale of values have been altered by our traffic with the machine.

But between the personality that was most effective in the technically immature environment of the tenth century and the type that is effective today, one may say that the first was subjectively conditioned, and that the second is more directly influenced by objective situations. These, at all events, seem to be the tendencies. In both types of personality there was an external standard of reference: but whereas the medieval man determined reality by the extent to which it agreed with a complicated tissue of beliefs, in the case of modern man the final arbiter of judgment is always a set of facts, recourse to which is equally open and equally satisfactory to all normally constituted organisms. With those that do not accept such a common substratum neither rational argument nor rational cooperation is possible. Moreover, matters that lie outside this verification in terms of fact have for the modern mind a lower order of reality, no matter how great the presumption, how strong the inner certainty, how passionate the interest. An angel and a high-frequency wave are equally invisible to the mass of mankind: but the reports of angels have come from only a limited number of human receptors, whereas by means of suitable apparatus communication between a sending and a receiving station can be inspected and checked up by any competent human being.

The technique of creating a neutral world of fact as distinguished from the raw data of immediate experience was the great general contribution of modern analytic science. This contribution was possibly second only to the development of our original language concepts, which built up and identified, with the aid of a common symbol, such as tree or man, the thousand confused and partial aspects of trees and men that occur in direct experience. Behind this technique, however, stands a special collective morality: a rational confidence in the work of other men, a loyalty to the reports of the senses, whether one likes them or not, a willingness to accept a competent and unbiased interpretation of the results. This recourse to a neutral judge and to a constructed body of law was a belated development in thought comparable to that which took place in morality when the blind conflicts between biassed men were replaced by the civil processes of justice. The collective process, even allowing for the accumulation of error and for the unconscious bias of the neutral instrument itself, gave a higher degree of certainty than the most forthright and subjectively satisfactory individual judgment.

The concept of a neutral world, untouched by man's efforts, indifferent to his activities, obdurate to his wish and supplication, is one of the great triumphs of man's imagination, and in itself it represents a fresh human value. Minds of the scientific order, even before Pythagoras, must have had intuitions of this world; but the habit of thought did not spread over any wide area until the scientific method and the machine technique had become common: indeed it does not begin to emerge with any clearness until the nineteenth century. The recognition of this new order is one of the main elements in the new objectivity. It is embodied in a common phrase which now rises to the lips of everyone when some accident or breakdown occurs in a process which lies outside everyone's immediate control: a leak in a gas tank in an airplane, a delay on a railroad: "That's that." "C'est ça." "So geht's." From machines that have broken down the same impersonal attitude begins to extend itself to the result of human negligence or human perversity: a badly cooked meal or the elopement of one's sweetheart. These events naturally often provoke stormy and uncontrollable emotional responses, but instead of magnifying the explosion and giving it more fuel, we tend to subject the response as well as the event to a common causal interpretation. The relative passiveness of machine-trained populations during periods when the industrial system itself has been disrupted, a passiveness that contrasts at times with the behavior of rural populations, is perhaps the less favorable side of the same objectivity.

Now in any complete analysis of character the "objective" personality is as much of an abstraction as the "romantic" personality. What we tend to call objective are those dispositions and attitudes which accord with the science and technics: but while one must take care not to confuse the objective or rational personality with the whole personality, it should be plain that the area of the first has increased—if only because it represents an adaptation indispensable to the running of the machine itself. And the adaptation in turn has further effects: a modulation of emphasis, a matter-of-factness, a reasonableness, a quiet assurance of a neutral realm in which the most obdurate differences can be understood, if not composed, is a mark of the emerging personality. The shrill, the violent, the vociferous, the purely animal tooth-baring and foot-stamping, paroxysms of uncritical self-love and uncontrolled hate—all these archaic qualities, which once characterized the leaders of men and their imitators, are now outside the style of our epoch: their recent revival and attempted sanctification is merely a symptom of that relapse into the raw primitive on which I dwelt a little while back. When one beholds these savage qualities today one has the sense of beholding a backward form of life, like the mastodon, or of witnessing the outburst of a demented personality. Between the fire of such low types and the ice of the machine one would have to choose the ice. Fortunately, our choice is not such a narrow one. In the development of the human character we have reached a point similar to that which we have attained in technics itself: the point at which we utilize the completest developments in science and technics to approach once more the organic. But here again: *our capacity to go beyond the machine rests upon our power to assimilate the machine. Until we have absorbed the lessons of objectivity, impersonality, neutrality, the lessons of the mechanical realm, we cannot go further in our development toward the more richly organic, the more profoundly human.*

III
ORIENTATION

1: The Dissolution of "The Machine"

What we call, in its final results, "the machine" was not, we have seen, the passive by-product of technics itself, developing through small ingenuities and improvements and finally spreading over the entire field of social effort. On the contrary, the mechanical discipline and many of the primary inventions themselves were the result of deliberate effort to achieve a mechanical way of life: the motive in back of this was not technical efficiency but holiness, or power over other men. In the course of development machines have extended these aims and provided a physical vehicle for their fulfillment.

Now, the mechanical ideology, which directed men's minds toward the production of machines, was itself the result of special circumstances, special choices and interests and desires. So long as other values were uppermost, European technology had remained relatively stable and balanced over a period of three or four thousand years. Men produced machines partly because they were seeking an issue from a baffling complexity and confusion, which characterized both action and thought: partly, too, because their desire for power, frustrated by the loud violence of other men, turned finally toward the neutral world of brute matter. Order had been sought before, again and again in other civilizations, in drill, regimentation, inflexible social regulations, the discipline of caste and custom: after the seventeenth century it was sought in a series of external instruments and engines. The Western European conceived of the machine because he wanted regularity, order, certainty, because he wished to reduce the movement of his fellows as well as the behavior of the environment to a more definite, calculable basis. But, more than an instrument of practical adjustment, the machine was, from 1750 on, a goal of desire. Though nominally designed to further the means of existence, the machine served the industrialist and the inventor and all the cooperating classes as an end. In a world of flux and disorder and precarious adjustment, the machine at least was seized upon as a finality.

If anything was unconditionally believed in and worshipped during the last two centuries, at least by the leaders and masters of society, it was the machine; for the machine and the universe were identified, linked together as they were by the formulae of the mathematical and physical sciences; and the service of the machine was the principal manifestation of faith and religion: the main motive of human action, and the source of most human goods. Only as a religion can one explain the compulsive nature of the urge toward mechanical development without regard for the actual outcome of the development in human relations themselves: even in departments where the results of mechanization were plainly disastrous, the most reasonable apologists nevertheless held that "the machine was here to stay"—by which they meant, not that history was irreversible, but that the machine itself was unmodifiable.

Today this unquestioned faith in the machine has been severely shaken. The absolute validity of the machine has become a conditioned validity: even Spengler, who has urged the men of his generation to become engineers and men of fact, regards that career as a sort of honorable suicide and looks forward to the period when the monuments of the machine civilization will be tangled masses of rusting iron and empty concrete shells. While for those of us who are more hopeful both of man's destiny and that of the machine, the machine is no longer the paragon of progress and the final expression of our desires: it is merely a series of instruments, which we will use in so far as they are serviceable to life at large, and which we will curtail where they infringe upon it or exist purely to support the adventitious structure of capitalism.

The decay of this absolute faith has resulted from a variety of causes. One of them is the fact that the instruments of destruction ingeniously contrived in the machine shop and the chemist's laboratory, have become in the hands of raw and dehumanized personalities a standing threat to the existence of organized society itself. Mechanical instruments of armament and offense, springing out of fear, have widened the grounds for fear among all the peoples of the world; and our insecurity against bestial, power-lusting men is too great a price to pay for relief from the insecurities of the natural environment. What is the use of conquering nature if we fall a prey to nature in the form of unbridled men? What is the use of equipping mankind with mighty powers to move and build and communicate, if the final result of this secure food supply and this excellent organization is to enthrone the morbid impulses of a thwarted humanity?

In the development of the neutral valueless world of science, and in the advance of the adaptive, instrumental functions of the machine, we have left to the untutored egoisms of mankind the control of the gigantic powers and engines technics has conjured into existence. In advancing too swiftly and heedlessly along the line of mechanical improvement we have failed to assimilate the machine and to co-ordinate it with human capacities and human needs; and by our social backwardness and our blind confidence that problems occasioned by the machine could be solved purely by mechanical means, we have outreached ourselves. When one subtracts from the manifest blessings of the machine the entire amount of energy and mind and time and resources devoted to the preparation for war—to say nothing of the residual burden of past wars—one realizes the net gain is dismayingly small, and with the advance of still more efficient means of inflicting death is becoming steadily smaller. Our failure here is the critical instance of a common failure all along the line.

The decay of the mechanical faith has, however, still another source: namely, the realization that the serviceability of machines has meant in the past serviceability to capitalist enterprise. We are now entering a phase of dissociation between capitalism and technics; and we begin to see with Thorstein Veblen that their respective interests, so far from being identical, are often at war, and that the human gains of technics have been forfeited by perversion in the interests of a pecuniary economy. We see in addition that many of the special gains in productivity which capitalism took credit for were in reality due to quite different agents—collective thought, cooperative action, and the general habits of order—virtues that have no necessary connection with capitalist enterprise. To perfect and extend the range of machines without perfecting and giving humane direction to the organs of social action and social control is to create dangerous tensions in the structure of society. Thanks to capitalism, the machine has been over-worked, over-enlarged, over-exploited because of the possibility of making money out of it. And the problem of integrating the machine in society is not merely a matter, as I have already pointed out, of making social institutions keep in step with the machine: the problem is equally one of altering the nature and the rhythm of the machine to fit the actual needs of the community. Whereas the physical sciences had first claim on the good minds of the past epoch, it is the biological and social sciences, and the political arts of industrial planning and regional planning and community planning that now most urgently need cultivation: once they begin to flourish they will awaken new interests and set new problems for the technologist. But the belief that the social dilemmas created by the machine can be solved merely by inventing more machines is today a sign of half-baked thinking which verges close to quackery.

These symptoms of social danger and decay, arising out of the very nature of the machine—its peculiar debts to warfare, mining, and finance—have weakened the absolute faith in the machine that characterized its earlier development.

At the same time, we have now reached a point in the development of technology itself where the organic has begun to dominate the machine. Instead of simplifying the organic, to make it intelligibly mechanical, as was necessary for the great eotechnic and paleotechnic inventions, we have begun to complicate the mechanical, in order to make it more organic: therefore more effective, more harmonious with our living environment. For our skill, perfected on the finger exercises of the machine, would be bored by the mere repetition of the scales and such childlike imbecilities: supported by the analytic methods and the skills developed in creating the machine, we can now approach the larger tasks of synthesis. In short, the machine is serving independently, in its neotechnic phase, as a point for a fresh integration in thought and social life.

While in the past the machine was retarded by its limited historic heritage, by its inadequate ideology, by its tendency to deny the vital and the organic, it is now transcending these limitations. And indeed, as our machines and our apparatus become more subtle, and the knowledge derived with their aid becomes more delicate and penetrating, the simple mechanical analysis of the universe made by the earlier physicists ceases to represent anything in which the scientist himself is now interested. The mechanical world-picture is dissolving. The intellectual medium in which the machine once spawned so rapidly is being altered at the same time that the social medium— the point of application—is undergoing a parallel change. Neither of these changes is yet dominant; neither is automatic or inevitable. But one can now say definitely, as one could not fifty years ago, that there is a fresh gathering of forces on the side of life. The claims of life, once expressed solely by the Romantics and by the more archaic social groups and institutions of society, are now beginning to be represented at the very heart of technics itself. Let us trace out some of the implications of this fact.

2: Toward an Organic Ideology

During the first period of mechanical advance, the application of simple mechanical analogies to complex organic phenomena helped the scientist to create a simple framework for experience in general, including manifestations of life. The "real" from this standpoint was that which could be measured and accurately defined; and the notion that reality might in fact be vague, complex, undefinable, perpetually a little obscure and shifty, did not go with the sure click and movement of machines.

Today this whole abstract framework is in process of reconstruction. Provisionally, it is as useful to say in science that a simple element is a limited kind of organism as it once was to say that an organism was a complicated kind of machine. "Newtonian physics," as Professor A. N. Whitehead says in Adventures of Ideas, "is based upon the independent individuality of every bit of matter. Each stone is conceived as fully describable apart from any reference to any other portion of matter. It might be alone in the universe, the sole occupant of uniform space. Also the stone could be adequately described without reference to past or future. It is to be conceived fully and adequately as wholly constituted within the present moment." These independent solid objects of Newtonian physics might move, touch each other, collide, or even, by a certain stretch of the imagination, act at a distance: but nothing could penetrate them except in the limited way that light penetrated translucent substances.

This world of separate bodies, unaffected by the accidents of history or of geographic location, underwent a profound change with the elaboration of the new concepts of matter and energy that went forward from Faraday and von Mayer through Clerk-Maxwell and Willard Gibbs and Ernest Mach to Planck and Einstein. The discovery that solids, liquids, and gases were phases of all forms of matter modified the very conception of substance, while the identification of electricity, light, and heat as aspects of a protean energy, and the final break-up of "solid" matter into particles of this same ultimate energy lessened the gap, not merely between various aspects of the physical world, but between the mechanical and the organic. Both matter in the raw and the more organized and internally self-sustaining organisms could be described as systems of energy in more or less stable, more or less complex, states of equilibrium.

In the seventeenth century the world was conceived as a series of independent systems. First, the dead world of physics, the world of matter and motion, subject to accurate mathematical description. Second, and inferior from the standpoint of factual analysis, was the world of living organisms, an ill-defined realm, subject to the intrusion of a mysterious entity, the vital principle. Third, the world of man, a strange being who was a mechanical automaton with reference to the world of physics, but an independent being with a destiny in heaven from the standpoint of the theologian. Today, instead of such a series of parallel systems, the world has conceptually become a single system: if it still cannot be unified in a single formula, it is even less conceivable without positing an underlying order that threads through all its manifestations. Those parts of reality that can be reduced to patent order, law, quantitative statement are no more real or ultimate than those parts which remain obscure and illusive: indeed, when applied at the wrong moment or in the wrong place or in a false context the exactness of the description may increase the error of interpretation.

All our really primary data are social and vital. One begins with life; and one knows life, not as a fact in the raw, but only as one is conscious of human society and uses the tools and instruments society has developed through history—words, symbols, grammar, logic, in short, the whole technique of communication and funded experience. The most abstract knowledge, the most impersonal method, is a derivative of this world of socially ordered values. And instead of accepting the Victorian myth of a struggle for existence in a blind and meaningless universe, one must, with Professor Lawrence Henderson, replace this with the picture of a partnership in mutual aid, in which the physical structure of matter itself, and the very distribution of elements on the earth's crust, their quantity, their solubility, their specific gravity, their distribution and chemical combination, are life-furthering and life-sustaining. Even the most rigorous scientific description of the physical basis of life indicates it to be internally teleological.

Now changes in our conceptual apparatus are rarely important or influential unless they are accompanied, more or less independently, by parallel changes in personal habits and social institutions. Mechanical time became important because it was re-enforced by the financial accountancy of capitalism: progress became important as a doctrine because visible improvements were being rapidly made in machines. So the organic approach in thought is important today because we have begun, here and there, to act on these terms even when unaware of the conceptual implications. This development has gone on in architecture from Sullivan and Frank Lloyd Wright to the new architects in Europe, and from Owen and Ebenezer Howard and Patrick Geddes in city design to the community planners in Holland, Germany, and Switzerland who have begun to crystallize in a fresh pattern the whole neotechnic environment. The humane arts of the physician and the psychologist and the architect, the hygienist and the community planner, have begun during the last few decades to displace the mechanical arts from their hitherto central position in our economy and our life. Form, pattern, configuration, organism, historical filiation, ecological relationship are concepts that work up and down the ladder of the sciences: the esthetic structure and the social relations are as real as the primary physical qualities that the sciences were once content to isolate. This conceptual change, then, is a widespread movement that is going on in every part of society: in part it arises out of the general resurgence of life—the care of children, the culture of sex, the return to wild nature and the re-newed worship of the sun—and in turn it gives intellectual re-enforce-ment to these spontaneous movements and activities. The very struc-ture of machines themselves, as I pointed out in describing the neo-technic phase, reflects these more vital interests. We now realize that the machines, at their best, are lame counterfeits of living organisms. Our finest airplanes are crude uncertain approximations compared with a flying duck: our best electric lamps cannot compare in effi-ciency with the light of the firefly: our most complicated automatic telephone exchange is a childish contraption compared with the nervous system of the human body.

This reawakening of the vital and the organic in every department undermines the authority of the purely mechanical. Life, which has always paid the fiddler, now begins to call the tune. Like The Walker in Robert Frost's poem, who found a nest of turtle eggs near a railroad track, we are armed for war:

> *The next machine that has the power to pass*
> *Will get this plasm on its polished brass.*

But instead of being confined to a resentment that destroys life in the act of hurling defiance, we can now act directly upon the nature of the machine itself, and create another race of these creatures, more effectively adapted to the environment and to the uses of life. At this point, one must go beyond Sombart's so far excellent analysis. Sombart pointed out, in a long list of contrasting productions and inventions, that the clue to modern technology was the displace-ment of the organic and the living by the artificial and the mechanical.

Within technology itself this process, in many departments, is being reversed: we are returning to the organic: at all events, we no longer regard the mechanical as all-embracing and all-sufficient.

Once the organic image takes the place of the mechanical one, one may confidently predict a slowing down of the tempo of research, the tempo of mechanical invention, and the tempo of social change, since a coherent and integrated advance must take place more slowly than a one-sided unrelated advance. Whereas the earlier mechanical world could be represented by the game of checkers, in which a similar series of moves is carried out by identical pieces, qualitatively similar, the new world must be represented by chess, a game in which each order of pieces has a different status, a different value, and a different function: a slower and more exacting game. By the same token, however, the results in technology and in society will be of a more solid nature than those upon which paleotechnic science congratulated itself: for the truth is that every aspect of the earlier order, from the slums in which it housed its workers to the towers of abstraction in which it housed its intellectuals, was jerrybuilt—hastily clapped together for the sake of immediate profits, immediate practical success, with no regard for the wider consequences and implications. The emphasis in future must be, not upon speed and immediate practical conquest, but upon exhaustiveness, inter-relationship, and integration. The co-ordination of our technical effort—such co-ordination and adjustment as is pictured for us in the physiology of the living organism—is more important than extravagant advances along special lines, and equally extravagant retardations along other lines, with a disastrous lack of balance and harmony between the various parts.

The fact is then that, partly thanks to the machine, we have now an insight into a larger world and a more comprehensive intellectual synthesis than that which was originally outlined in our mechanical ideology. We can now see plainly that power, work, regularity, are adequate principles of action only when they cooperate with a humane scheme of living: that any mechanical order we can project must fit into the larger order of life itself. Beyond the necessary intellectual reconstruction, which is already going on in both science and technics,

we must build up more organic centers of faith and action in the arts
of society and in the discipline of the personality: this implies a re-
orientation that will take us far beyond the immediate province of
technics itself. These are matters—matters touching the building of
communities, the conduct of groups, the development of the arts of
communication and expression, the education and the hygiene of
the personality—that I purpose to take up in another book. Here I
will confine attention to co-ordinate readjustments which are clearly
indicated and already partly formulated and enacted in the realm
of technics and industry.

3: The Elements of Social Energetics

Let us examine the implications of neotechnic developments, within
the machine itself, upon our economic objectives, upon the organization of work, upon the direction of industry and the goals of consumption, upon the emerging social purposes of the neotechnic phase
of civilization.

First: the economic objectives.

In the course of capitalistic enterprise, which accompanied the
widespread introduction of machines and machine-methods in the
fifteenth and sixteenth centuries, the focus of industry shifted from
the craft guild to the merchant guild or the livery company or the
company of merchant adventurers, or to the special organization for
exploiting patent monopolies. The means of exchange usurped the
function and meaning of the things that were exchanged: money
itself became a commodity and money-getting became a specialized
form of activity. Under capitalism profit reigned as the main economic objective; and profit became the decisive factor in all industrial enterprise. Inventions that promised profits, industries that
produced profits, were fostered. The reward of capital, if not the
first claim upon productive enterprise, was at all events the dominating one: the service of the consumer and the support of the worker
were entirely secondary. Even in a period of crisis and breakdown,
such as that capitalism is still in the midst of at the moment I
write, dividends continue to be paid to rentiers out of past accumulation while the industry itself often operates at a loss, or the mass

of workers are turned out to starve. Sometimes profits were obtained by lowering the costs and spreading the product: but if they could be had only by offering inferior or adulterated goods—as in the sale of medical nostrums or the slum housing of the underpaid worker—health and well-being were sacrificed to gain. The community, instead of receiving a full return for its goods and services, permitted a portion of the product to be diverted for the private gratification of the holders of land and capital. These holders of land and capital, backed up by the law and all the instruments of government, determined privately and solely in accordance with the canon of profit what should be produced and how much and where and how and by whom and on what terms.

In the economic analysis of the society that grew up on this basis, the three main terms in industrial activity were production, distribution, and consumption. Profits were to be increased by cheaper production, by wider and multifold distribution, and by a steadily rising standard of consumptive expenditure, with—sometimes in lieu of that, sometimes accompanying it—an enlarging market of consumers. Saving labor, or cheapening labor by a superiority of bargaining power—obtained by withholding land from the laborer and monopolizing the new instruments of production—were the two chief means, from the capitalist's standpoint, of increasing the margin of profits. Saving labor by rationalization was a real improvement which bettered everything but the position of the laborer. The stimulation of the demand for goods was the chief means of increasing the turnover: hence the problem of capitalism was essentially not to satisfy needs but to create demands. And the attempt to represent(this process of private aggrandizement and class-advantage as a natural and socially beneficent one was perhaps the main labor of political economists during the nineteenth century.

When one examines economic activities from the standpoint of the employment of energy and the service of human life, this whole financial structure of production and consumption turns out to have mainly a superstitious basis. At the bottom of the structure are farmer and peasant, who during the entire course of the industrial revolution, which their increase of the food supply has made possible, have scarcely ever received an adequate return for their products—at least on the basis of pecuniary accountancy by which the rest of this society was run. Furthermore: what are called gains in capitalist economics often turn out, from the standpoint of social energetics, to be losses; while the real gains, the gains upon which all the activities of life, civilization, and culture ultimately depend were either counted as losses, or were ignored, because they remained outside the commercial scheme of accountancy.

What are, then, the essentials of the economic processes in relation to energy and to life? The essential processes are conversion, production, consumption, and creation. In the first two steps energy is seized and prepared for the sustenance of life. In the third stage, life is supported and renewed in order that it may wind itself up, so to speak, on the higher levels of thought and culture, instead of being short-circuited at once back into the preparatory functions. Normal human societies exhibit all four stages of the economic processes: but their absolute quantities and their proportions vary with the social milieu.

Conversion has to do with the utilization of the environment as a source of energy. The prime fact of all economic activity, from that of the lower organisms up to the most advanced human cultures, is the conversion of the sun's energies: this transformation depends upon the heat-conserving properties of the atmosphere, upon the geological processes of uplift and erosion and soil-building, upon the conditions of climate and local topography, and—most important of all—upon the green leaf reaction in growing plants. This seizure of energy is the original source of all our gains: on a purely energetic interpretation of the process, all that happens after this is a dissipation of energy—a dissipation that may be retarded, that may be dammed up, that may be temporarily diverted by human ingenuity, but in the long run cannot be averted. All the permanent monuments of human culture are attempts, by using more attentuated physical means of preserving and transmitting this energy, to avert the hour of ultimate extinction. The most important conquest of energy was man's original discovery and utilization of fire; after that, the most significant transformation of the environment came through the cultivation of the grain-bearing grasses, the vegetables, and the domestic animals. Indeed, the enormous increase in population which took place at the beginning of the nineteenth century, *before* the machine had made any appreciable change in agriculture, was due to the opening of immense areas of free land for grain cultivation and cattle raising and the better provision of winter fodder crops, combined with the addition of three new energy crops—sugar cane, sugar beet, and potato—to the diet of the industrial population.

The mechanical conversion of energy is second in importance to the organic conversion. But in the development of technics the invention of the water-wheel, the water-turbine, the steam engine, and the gas engine multiplied the energies that were available to man through the use of foods grown for himself and his domestic animals. Without the magnification of human energy made possible through this series of prime movers, our apparatus of production and transport could not have reached the gigantic scale it attained in the nineteenth century. All the further steps in the economic process depend upon the original act of conversion: the level of achievement can never rise higher than the level of the energy originally converted, and just as only an insignificant part of the sun's energy available is utilized in conversion, so only a small part of this, in turn, finally is utilized in consumption and creation.

Conversion lifts the energy available to a peak: from that point on energy runs down hill, in gathering and shaping the raw materials, in transporting supplies and products, and in the processes of consumption itself. Not until the economic process reaches the stage of creation—not until it supplies the human animal with more energy than he needs to maintain his physical existence, and not until still other energies are transformed into the more durable media of art and science and philosophy, of books, buildings and symbols—is there anything that can be called, even within a limited span of time, a gain. At one end of the process is the conversion of the free energy of nature and its transformation into forms useable by agriculture and technology: at the other end of the process is the conversion of the intermediate, preparatory products into human subsistence, and into those cultural forms that are useable by succeeding generations of men.

The amount of energy available for the final process depends upon two facts: how much energy is converted by agriculture and technics at the beginning, and how much of that energy is effectively applied and conserved in transmission. Even the crudest society has some surplus. But under the capitalist system the main use of this surplus is to serve as profits which are incentives to capital investments, which in turn increase production. Hence two massive and recurrent facts in modern capitalism: first, an enormous over-expansion of plant and equipment. Thus the Hoover Committee on the Elimination of Waste in Industry found, for example, that clothing factories in the United States are about 45 per cent larger than necessary; printing establishments are from 50 to 150 per cent over-equipped; and the shoe industry has a capacity.twice that of actual production. Second: an excessive diversion of energy and man-power into sales promotion and distribution. Whereas only ten per cent of the working population in the United States was engaged in transporting and distributing the commodities produced in 1870, the proportion had risen to 25 per cent in 1920. Other means of utilizing the surplus, such as the cultural and educational bequests of various philanthropies, relieve some of the burden of inane waste from both the individual and from industrial society: but there is no capitalist theory of non-profit-making enterprises and non-consumable goods. These functions exist accidentally, by the grace of the philanthropist: they have no real place in the system. Yet it should be plain that as society becomes technically mature and civilized, the area occupied by the surplus must become progressively wider: it will be greater than it occupied under capitalism or under those more primitive non-capitalist civilizations which—as was pregnantly demonstrated by Radhakamal Mukerjee—capitalist economics so inadequately describes.

The permanent gain that emerges from the whole economic process is in the relatively non-material elements in culture—in the social heritage itself, in the arts and sciences, in the traditions and processes of technology, or directly in life itself, in those real enrichments that come from the free exploitation of organic energy in thought and action and emotional experience, in play and adventure and drama and personal development—gains that last through memory and communication beyond the immediate moment in which they are enjoyed. In short, as John Ruskin put it, *There is no Wealth but Life;* and what we call wealth is in fact wealth only when it is a sign of potential or actual vitality.

An economic process that did not produce this margin for leisure, enjoyment, absorption, creative activity, communication and transmission would completely lack human meaning and reference. In the histories of human groups there are of course periods, periods of starvation, periods of flood and earthquake and war, when man fights a losing fight with his environment, and does not even secure bare physical survival; and there are moments when the complete social process is brutally cut short. But even in the most perverse and degraded forms of life, there is an aspect that corresponds, vitally and psychally speaking, to "creation," and even in the most inadequate forms of production, such as that which prevailed during the paleotechnic phase, there remains a surplus not arrogated by industry. Whether this surplus goes to increase the preparatory processes, or whether it is to be spent on creation, is a choice that cannot be automatically decided; and the tendency in capitalist society to put it back quickly into the preparatory processes, and to make possible increased production by applying pressure to consumption, is merely a further indication of its absence of social criteria.

The real significance of the machine, socially speaking, does not consist either in the multiplication of goods or the multiplication of wants, real or illusory. Its significance lies in the gains of energy through increased conversion, through efficient production, through balanced consumption, and through socialized creation. The test of economic success does not, therefore, lie in the industrial process alone, and it cannot be measured by the amount of horsepower converted or by the amount commanded by an individual user: for the important factors here are not quantities but ratios: ratios of mechanical effort to social and cultural results. A society in which production and consumption completely cancelled out the gains of conversion—in which people worked to live and lived to work—would remain socially inefficient, even if the entire population were constantly employed, and adequately fed, clothed, and sheltered.

The ultimate test of an efficient industry is the ratio between productive means and the achieved ends. Hence a society with a low scale of conversion but with a high amount of creation is humanly speaking superior to a society with an enormous panoply of converters and a small and inadequate army of creators. By the ruthless pillage of the food-producing territories of Asia and Africa, the Roman Empire appropriated far more energy than Greece, with its sparse abstemious dietary and its low standard of living. But Rome produced no poem, no statue, no original architecture, no work of science, no philosophy comparable to the Odyssey, the Parthenon, the works of sixth and fifth century sculptors, and the science of Pythagoras, Euclid, Archimedes, Hero: and so the quantitative grandeur and luxury and power of the Romans, despite their extraordinary capacity as engineers, remained relatively meaningless: even for the continued development of technics the work of the Greek mathematicians and physicists was more important.

This is why no working ideal for machine production can be based solely on the gospel of work: still less can it be based upon an uncritical belief in constantly raising the quantitative standard of consumption. If we are to achieve a purposive and cultivated use of the enormous energies now happily at our disposal, we must examine in detail the processes that lead up to the final state of leisure, free activity, creation. It is because of the lapse and mismanagement of these processes that we have not reached the desirable end; and it is because of our failure to frame a comprehensive scheme of ends that we have not succeeded in achieving even the beginnings of social efficiency in the preparatory work.

How is this margin to be achieved and how is it to be applied? Already we are faced with political and moral problems as well as technological ones. There is nothing in the nature of the machine as such, nothing in the training of the technician as such, that will provide us with a sufficient answer. We shall of course need his help: but in turn *he* will need help from other quarters of the compass, far beyond the province of technology.

4: Increase Conversion!

Modern technics began in Western Civilization with an increased capacity for conversion. While society faces a fairly imminent shortage of petroleum and perhaps natural gas, and while the known coal beds of the world give no longer promise of life, at the present rates of consumption, than three thousand years, we face no serious energy problem that we cannot solve even with our present equipment, provided that we utilize to the full our scientific resources. Apart from the doubtful possibility of harnessing inter-atomic energy, there is the much nearer one of utilizing the sun's energy directly in sun-converters or of utilizing the difference in temperature between the lower depths and the surface of the tropical seas: there is likewise the possibility of applying on a wide scale new types of wind turbine, like the rotor: indeed, once an efficient storage battery was available the wind alone would be sufficient, in all probability, to supply any reasonable needs for energy.

Along with the renewed use through electricity of wind and water one must put the destructive distillation of coal, near the pitheads, in the new types of coke-oven. This not merely saves enormous amounts in energy now spent in transporting the fuel from the place where it is mined to the place where it is used, but it also conserves the precious compounds that now escape into the air in the wasteful individual furnaces. Theoretically, however, such economies of energy only lead to wider consumption and so to more rapid utilization of the very thing we wish to conserve: hence the necessity for making a socialized monopoly of all such raw materials and resources. The private monopoly of coal beds and oil wells is an intolerable anachronism—as intolerable as would be the monopoly of sun, air, running water. Here the objectives of a price economy and a social economy cannot be reconciled; and the common ownership of the means of converting energy, from the wooded mountain regions where the streams have their sources down to the remotest petroleum wells is the sole safeguard to their effective use and conservation. Only by increasing the amount of energy available, or, when the amount is restricted, by economizing more cunningly in its application, shall we be in a position to eliminate freely the basest forms of drudgery.

What is true for mechanical power production is likewise true for organic forms of power production, such as the growing of foods and the extraction of raw materials from the soil. In this department capitalistic society has confused ownership with security of tenure and continuity of effort, and in the very effort to foster ownership while maintaining the speculative market it has destroyed security of tenure. It is the latter condition that is necessary for conservative farming; and not until the community itself holds the land will the position of the farmer be a desirable one. The negative side of this socialization of the land—namely, the purchase of marginal land, unfit for any other purpose than forest growth—has already been taken up, for example, by the State of New York. It remains to accomplish a similar end on the positive side by taking over and appropriately planning for maximum cultivation and enjoyment the good agricultural lands.

Such ownership and planning by the community do not necessarily mean large-scale farming: for the efficient economic units differ with the type of farming, and the large mechanized units suitable to the cultivation of the wheatlands of the prairies are in fact inappropriate to other types of farming. Neither does such a system of rationalization inevitably mean the extinction of the small family farming group, with the skill and initiative and general intelligence that distinguishes the farmer favorably from the over-specialized factory worker of the old style. But the permanent zoning of certain areas for certain types of agriculture, and the experimental determination of the types of crop appropriate to a particular region or a particular section are matters that cannot be left to guess, chance, or blind individual initiative: they are, on the contrary, complicated technical questions in which objective answers are possible. In long-settled areas, like the various wine-growing sections of France, soil utilization surveys will probably only confirm existing types of effort: but wherever there is a question of choice between types of use, the decision cannot be left to the chance interests of individuals. The first step toward rationalization in agriculture is the common ownership of the land. Such ownership prevailed in Europe under customary forms down to the nineteenth century in certain regions; and its restoration involves no breach whatever with the essential foundations of rural life.

The private appropriation and exploitation of the land, indeed, must be looked upon as a transitory state, peculiar to capitalism, between customary local agriculture based upon the common needs of the small local community and a rationed world agriculture, based upon the cooperative resources of the entire planet, considered as a federation of balanced regions. The fact that, except in times of extreme scarcity, the farmer is pauperized or ruined by the abundance of his crops only emphasizes the point that a more stable basis for agricultural production must be found: a basis that does not rely upon the individual guesses of the farmer, the caprices of nature, and the speculative fluctuations of the world market. Within any given period price tends to vary inversely with the quantity available: here as elsewhere monetary values disappear toward zero as vital values and energies rise. Hence the need for rationing, for stable crops, and for an altogether new system of determining price and marketability. I shall go into this last point presently. It is enough to point out here that with the development of balanced economic regions, agricultural production will be related to a stable local market, the sudden gluts and shortages that arise with transportation to distant centers will disappear, and further to regularize production, a good part of the more delicate crops will be grown in small units, possibly, as in Holland, under glass, near the place of consumption.

To increase conversion, then, is no simple matter of merely mining coal or building more dynamos. It involves the social appropriation of natural resources, the replanning of agriculture and the maximum utilization of those regions in which kinetic energy in the form of sun, wind, and running water is abundantly available. The socialization of these sources of energy is a condition of their effective and purposive use.

5: Economize Production!

The application of power to production and the employment of quick and relatively tireless machines to perform manual movement and the organization of rapid transport and the concentration of work into factories were the chief means adopted during the nineteenth century to increase the quantity of commodities available. And the goal of this development within the factory was the complete substitution of non-human power for man power, of mechanical skill for human skill, of automatons for workers, in every department where this was possible. Where the absence of human feelings or intelligence did not manifest itself in an inferiority of the product itself, that goal was a legitimate one.

The mechanical elements in production were rationalized much more rapidly than the human elements. In fact, one might almost say that the human elements were irrationalized at the same time; for the stimuli to production, human fellowship, an *esprit de corps*, the hope of advancement and mastery, the appreciation of the entire process of work itself, were all reduced or wiped out at the very moment that the work itself, through its subdivision, ceased to give any independent gratification. Only the pecuniary interest in production remained; and the majority of mankind, unlike the avaricious and ambitious spirits who marched to the head of industry, are apparently so irresponsive to this pecuniary stimulus that the directing classes relied upon the lash of starvation, rather than upon the pleasures of surfeit, to drive them back to the machine.

Collective instruments of production were created and used, without the benefit of a collective will and a collective interest. That, to begin with, was a serious handicap upon productive efficiency. The workers grudged the efforts they gave to the machine, applied themselves with half a mind, loitered and loafed when there was an opportunity to escape the eye of the foreman or the taskmaster, sought to give as little as they could in return for as much wages as they could get. So far from attempting to combat these sources of inefficiency, the enterprisers sanctioned it by relieving the worker of such autonomy and responsibility as might naturally adhere to the job, by insisting upon speed for the sake of cheapness without regard for the excellence of workmanship, and by managing industry with an eye solely upon the maximum cash return. There were exceptions in every industry; but they did not establish the main line.

Not appreciating the gain to efficiency from collective loyalty and collective interest and a strong common drive, the great industrialists did their best to browbeat any of these incipient responses out of the worker: by lockouts, by ruthless warfare in strikes, by hard bargains in wages and by callous layoffs during periods of slack work the typical employers of labor did their ignorant best to decrease the efficiency of the workers and throw sand in the works. These tactics greatly increased the labor turnover and therefore lowered the internal efficiency of operation: even such a moderate improvement in the wage scale as Ford introduced in Detroit had a powerful effect in lessening such losses. But what shall one say to the efficiency of a productive system in which strikes and lockouts in the United States, according to Polakov, at the beginning of the last decade, averaged 54 million man-days of idleness per year? The loss and inefficiency due to the failure to create a cooperative pattern of human relations which would supplement that of the machine industry itself cannot be estimated: but the success of such occasional mutations within the capitalist system as the Cadbury Cocoa works at Bourneville, the Godin steel works at Guise—an adaptation of Fourier's scheme for a cooperative phalanstery—and the Dennison paper manufacturing works at Framingham, Massachusetts, gives a slight indication of what our total efficiency would have been had social relations themselves been rationalized at the time the machine was introduced. It is evident, at all events, that a good part of our mechanical adroitness has been annulled by social friction, waste, and unnecessary human wear and tear. Testimony to that effect comes from the production engineers themselves.

At the end of the nineteenth century a new attack upon the problem of efficiency in production was made within the factory: it was no accident perhaps that the distinguished engineer who initiated it was also the co-inventor of a new high-speed tool steel, a characteristic neotechnic advance. Instead of studying the machine as an isolated unit, Taylor studied the worker himself as an element in production. By a close factual study of his movements, Taylor was able to add to the labor output per man without adding to his physical burden. The time and motion studies that Taylor and his followers introduced have now with the development of serial processes and greater automatism, become somewhat outmoded: their importance lay in the fact that they directed attention to the industrial process as a whole and treated the worker as an integral element in it. Their weakness lay in the fact that they accepted the aims of capitalist production as fixed, and they were compelled to rely upon a narrow pecuniary incentive—with piecework production and bonuses—to achieve the mechanical gains that were possible.

The next step toward the genuine rationalization of industry lies in widening the interests and increasing the social incentives to production. On one hand, this means the reduction of trivial and degrading forms of work: it likewise means the elimination of products that have no real social use, since there is no form of cruelty for a rational human being worse than making him produce goods that have no human value: picking oakum is by comparison an edifying task. In addition, the stimulation of invention and initiative within the industrial process, the reliance upon group activity and upon intimate forms of social approval, and the transformation of work into education, and of the social opportunities of factory production into effective forms of political action—all these incentives toward a humanly controlled and effectively directed industrial production await the formulation of non-capitalist modes of enterprise. Taylorism, though it had within its technique the germ of a revolutionary change in industry, was reduced to a minor instrument in almost every country except Russia. But it is precisely in the political and psychological relations of the worker to the industry that the most effective economies have still to be made. This has been excellently illustrated in an experiment in a Westinghouse plant described by Professor Elton Mayo. By paying attention to the conditions of work and by providing rest periods, the efficiency of a group of workers was steadily raised. After a certain period of experiment, the group was put back in the original condition of work without rest periods: still the output was greater than it had been originally. What had happened? There was a feeling among the operatives, according to the observer, that "better output is in some way related to the distinctively pleasanter, freer, and happier working conditions." This is a long stage beyond Taylor's original mechanical motion study. And it points to a factor of efficiency in socialized industry, in which the worker himself is fully respected, which capitalism at its most enlightened best can scarcely more than touch. (Is not this human factor perhaps one of the reasons why small scale industry—in addition to its lower overhead—can still often compete with large scale industry, where monopoly does not favor the latter?)

Meanwhile, modern production has added enormously to the productive output without adding a single horsepower or a single machine or a single workman. What have been the means? On one hand there have been great gains through mechanical articulation within the factory, and through the closer organization of raw materials, transport, storage, and utilization in the factory itself. By timing, working out economic sequences, creating an orderly pattern of activity, the engineer has added enormously to the collective product. By transferring power from human organisms to machines, he has decreased the number of variable factors and integrated the process as a whole. These are the gains of organization and administration. The other set of gains has come through standardization and serial production. This involves the reduction of a whole group of different articles, in which differences did not correspond to essential qualities, to a limited number of types: once these types can be established and suitable machines devised to processing and manufacturing them the process can approach more and more closely to automatism. The dangers here lie in premature standardization; and in making assembled objects—like automobiles—so completely standardized that they cannot be improved without a wholesale scrapping of the plant. This was the costly mistake that was made in the Ford Model T. But in all the ranges of production where typification is possible large productive economies can be achieved by that method alone.

One returns to the illustration originally used by Babbage. The stone could be moved without skill or organized effort by exerting 753 pounds of effort: or it might be moved, by adapting appropriately every part of the environment, by using only twenty-two pounds. In its crude state, industry prides itself upon its gross use of power and machinery. In its advanced state it rests upon rational organization, social control, physiological and psychological understanding. In the first case, it relies upon the external exercise of power in its political relations: indeed, it prides itself upon surmounting the friction which with such superb ineptitude it creates. In the second state, no part of the works can remain immune to criticism and rational criteria: the goal is no longer as much production as is compatible with the canons of private enterprise and private profit and individual money-incentives: it is rather efficient production for social uses no matter how drastically these sacred canons must be revised or extirpated.

In a word, to economize production, we cannot begin or end with the physical machines and utilities themselves, nor can efficient production begin and end in the individual factory or industry. The process involves an integration of the worker, the industrial function, and the product, just as it involves a further co-ordination between the sources of supply and the final consumptive outlets. At hardly any point in our present system of production have we begun to utilize the latent energies that are available through organization and social control: at best, here and there, we have just begun to sample such efficiencies.

If we have only begun to utilize the latent energies of the personnel, it is equally true that the geographic distribution of industries, hitherto governed by accidental choices and opportunities, has still to be worked out rationally in terms of the world's resources and the re-settlement of the world's population into the areas marked as favorable for human living. Here, through economic regionalism, a new series of economies offers itself.

The accidents of original manufacture or of the original location of resources cannot continue as guiding factors in growth when new sources of supply and new distribution of markets are recognized.

Moreover, the neotechnic distribution of power makes for economic regionalism: the concentration of population in the coal towns and the port towns was a mark of a haphazardly organized labor supply and of the high cost of coal transportation. One of the large possibilities for economy here lies in the abolition of cross-hauls: the familiar process of carrying coals to Newcastle. Traders and middlemen gain by lengthening the distance in space and time between the producer and the ultimate consumer. Under a rationally planned distribution of industry, this parasitism in transit would be reduced to a minimum. And as the knowledge of modern technics spreads, the special advantages in skill and organization and science, once enjoyed by a few countries alone, by England during the nineteenth century above all, tend to become the common property of mankind at large: for ideas are not stopped by customs barriers or freight rates. Our modern world, transporting knowledge and skill, has diminished the need for transporting goods: St. Louis's shoes are as good as New England's, and French textiles are as good as English. In a balanced economy, regional production of commonplace commodities becomes rational production; and inter-regional exchange becomes the export of the surplus from regions of increment to regions of scarcity, or the exchange of special materials and skills—like Tungsten, manganese, fine china, lenses—not universally found or developed throughout the world. But even here the advantages of a particular place may remain temporary. While American and German camembert cheese is still vastly inferior to the French variety, the gruyère cheese produced in Wisconsin compares favorably with that produced in Switzerland. With the growth of economic regionalism, the advantages of modern industry will be spread, not chiefly by transport—as in the nineteenth century—but by local development.

The prime examples of conscious economic regionalism up to the present have come from countries like Ireland and Denmark, or states like Wisconsin, where the occupations were predominantly agricultural, and where a flourishing economic life depended upon an intelligent exploitation of all the regional resources. But economic regionalism does not aim at complete self-sufficiency: even under the most primitive conditions no region has ever been economically self-sufficient in all respects. On the other hand, economic regionalism does aim at combating the evil of over-specialization: since whatever the temporary commercial advantages of such specialization it tends to impoverish the cultural life of a region and, by placing all its eggs in one basket, to make precarious ultimately its economic existence. Just as every region has a potential balance of animal life and vegetation, so it has a potential social balance between industry and agriculture, between cities and farms, between built-up spaces and open spaces. A region entirely specialized for a single resource, or covered from boundary line to boundary line by a solid area of houses and streets, is a defective environment, no matter how well its trade may temporarily flourish. Economic regionalism is necessary to provide for a varied social life, as well as to provide for a balanced economy.

Plainly, a good part of the activity and business and power of the modern world, in which the nineteenth century took so much pride, was the result of disorganization, ignorance, inefficiency and social ineptitude. But the spread of technical knowledge, standardized methods, and scientifically controlled performances diminishes the need for transportation: in the new economy the old system of regional over-specialization will become the exception rather than the rule. Even today England is no longer the workshop of the world, and New England is no longer the workshop of America. And as mechanical industry becomes more highly rationalized and more finely adapted to the environment, a varied and many-sided industrial life tends to develop within each natural human region.

To achieve all these possible gains in production takes us far beyond the individual factory or industry, far beyond the current tasks of the administrator or engineer: it requires the services of the geographer and the regional planner, the psychologist, the educator, the sociologist, the skilled political administrator. Perhaps Russia alone at present has the necessary framework for this planning in its fundamental institutions; but to one degree or another, pushed by the necessity for creating order out of the existing chaos and disorganization, other countries are moving in the same direction: the

Zuyder Zee reclamation in Holland, for example, is an example of the multifold rationalization of industry and agriculture and the building up of economic regional units here indicated.

The older modes of production have exploited only the superficial processes that were capable of being mechanized and externally ordered: whereas a bolder social economy will touch every aspect of the industrial complex. Complete organization of the mechanical elements, with ignorance, accident, and uncriticized custom dominant in society as a whole, was the formula of capitalistic enterprise during its earlier phases. That formula belongs to the past. It achieved only a small part of the potential production that even the crude machine age of the past was capable of, provided that it could have removed the frictions and contradictions and cross-purposes that perpetually impeded the flow of goods from source to mouth. To achieve efficiency in the past was as self-defeating a task as Carlyle's famous dilemma—given a band of thieves to produce an honesty out of their united action. In detail, we will doubtless carry over many admirable practices and rational arrangements derived from capitalism: but it is entirely doubtful, so deep are the dissonances, so inevitable are the frictions, that we shall carry over capitalist society itself. Humanly speaking, it has worn out its welcome. We need a system more safe, more flexible, more adaptable, and finally more life-sustaining than that constructed by our narrow and one-sided financial economy. Its efficiency was a mere shadow of real efficiency, its wasteful power was a poor substitute for order; its feverish productivity and its screaming breakdowns, wastes, and jams were low counterfeits of a functional economy that could really profit by modern technics.

6: Normalize Consumption!

Whereas we must maximize conversion, in order to have surplus energies ready to fulfill existing wants, and to be prepared for unexpected needs, it does not follow that we must also maximize production along the existing lines of effort. The aimless expansion of production is in fact the typical disease of capitalism in its application of modern technics: for since it failed to establish norms it had no definite measure for its productive achievement and no possible goals, except those erected by custom and accidental desire.

The expansion of the machine during the past two centuries was accompanied by the dogma of increasing wants. Industry was directed not merely to the multiplication of goods and to an increase in their variety: it was directed toward the multiplication of the desire for goods. We passed from an economy of need to an economy of acquisition. The desire for more material satisfactions of the nature furnished by mechanized production kept up with and partly cancelled out the gains in productivity. Needs became nebulous and indirect: to satisfy them appropriately under the capitalist criterion one must gratify them with profitable indirectness through the channels of sale. The symbol of price made direct seizure and gratification vulgar: so that finally the farmer who produced enough fruit and meat and vegetables to satisfy his hunger felt a little inferior to the man who, producing these goods for a market, could buy back the inferior products of the packing house and the cannery. Does that exaggerate the reality? On the contrary, it hardly does justice to it. Money became the symbol of reputable consumption in every aspect of living, from art and education to marriage and religion.

Max Weber pointed out the extraordinary departure of the new doctrines of industrialism from the habits and customs of the greater part of mankind under the more parsimonious system of production that prevailed in the past. The aim of traditional industry was not to increase the number of wants, but to satisfy the standards of a particular class. Even today, among the poor, the habits of this past linger on along with relics of magic and primitive medicine: for an increase in wages, instead of being used to raise the worker's standard of expenditure, is sometimes used to secure respite from work, or to provide the wherewithal for a spree which leaves the worker in exactly the same physical and social state he was in before beginning it. The notion of employing money to escape one's class, and of spending money conspicuously in order to register the fact that one has escaped, did not come into existence in society at large until a fairly late stage in the development of capitalism, although it manifested itself in the upper ranks at the very beginning of the modern régime.

The dogma of increasing wants, like so many other dogmas of industrialism and democracy, first appeared in the counting house and the court, and then filtered down into the rest of society. When abstract counters in gold or paper became the symbols of power and wealth, men began to value a form of commodity that had in fact no natural limits. The absence of normal standards of acquisition first manifested itself among the successful bankers and merchants; yet even here these standards lingered on far into the nineteenth century in the conception of retiring from business after achieving a competence—that is, the standards of one's class. The absence of a customary norm of consumption was most conspicuous in the extravagant life of the courts. To externalize the desire for power, wealth, and privilege, the princes of the Renascence lavished upon private luxury and display enormous amounts of money. They themselves, unless they happened to rise from the merchant class, did not earn this money: they were forced therefore to beg, borrow, extort, steal, or pillage it; and truth to tell, they left none of these possibilities unexplored. Once the machine began to increase the money-making capacities of industry, these limits were extended and the level of expenditure was raised for the entire society. This phase of capitalism was accompanied, as I have already pointed out, by a widespread breakdown of social institutions: hence the private individual often sought to compensate by egocentric getting and spending for the absence of collective institutions and a collective aim. The wealth of nations was devoted to the private gratification of individuals: the marvels of collective enterprise and cooperation that the machine brought into play left the community itself impoverished.

Despite the natural egalitarian tendency of mass production, a great gap continued to exist between the various economic classes: this gap was glibly accounted for, in terms of Victorian economics, by a differentiation between necessities, comforts, and luxuries. The bare necessities were the lot of the mass of workers. The middle classes, in addition to having their necessities satisfied on an ampler scale than the workers, were supported by comforts: while the rich possessed in addition—and this made them more fortunate—luxuries. Yet there was a contradiction. Under the doctrine of increasing wants the mass of mankind was supposed to adopt for itself the ultimate goal of a princely standard of expenditure. There existed nothing less than a moral obligation to demand larger quantities and more various kinds of goods—the only limit to this obligation being the persistent unwillingness of the capitalist manufacturer to give the worker a sufficient share of the industrial income to make an effective demand. (At the height of the last wave of financial expansion in the United States the capitalist sought to solve this paradox by loaning money for increased consumption—installment purchase —without raising wages, lowering prices, or decreasing his own excessive share in the national income: a device which would never have occurred to the more sober Harpagons of the seventeenth century.)

The historic mistakes of men are never so plausible and so dangerous as when they are embodied in a formal doctrine, capable of being expressed in a few catchwords. The dogma of increasing wants, and the division of consumption into necessities, comforts, and luxuries, and the description of the economic process as leading to the universalizing of more expensive standards of consumption *in terms of machine-made goods*—all these beliefs have been largely taken for granted, even by many of those who have opposed the outright injustices and the more flagrant inequalities of the capitalist economic system. The doctrine was put, with a classic fatuousness and finality, by the Hoover Committee's report on Recent Economic Changes in the United States. "The survey has proved conclusively," says the report, "what has long been held theoretically to be true, that wants are almost insatiable; that one want makes way for another. The conclusion is that economically we have a boundless field before us; that there are new wants which will make way endlessly for newer wants, as fast as they are satisfied."

When one abandons class standards of consumption and examines the facts themselves from the standpoint of the vital processes that are to be served, one finds that there is not a single element in these doctrines that can be retained.

First of all: vital wants are all necessarily limited. Just as the organism itself does not continue to grow beyond the norm of its species, a norm established within relatively narrow limits, so neither can any particular function of life be satisfied by limitless indulgence. The body does not require more than a limited number of calories of food per day. If it functions adequately on three meals a day, it does not become three times as strong or effective on nine meals: on the contrary, it is likely to suffer from indigestion and constipation. If the intensity of amusement is tripled in a circus by the use of three rings instead of one there are few other circumstances in which this rule holds: the value of various stimuli and interests is not increased by quantitative multiplication, nor yet, beyond a certain point, by endless variety. A variety of products which perform similar functions is like omnivorousness in diet: a useful factor of safety. But this does not alter the essential fact of stability of desire and demand. A harem of a thousand wives may satisfy the vanity of an oriental monarch; but what monarch is sufficiently well endowed by nature to satisfy the harem?

Healthy activity requires restriction, monotony, repetition, as well as change, variety, and expansion. The querulous boredom of a child that possesses too many toys is endlessly repeated in the lives of the rich who, having no pecuniary limit to the expression of their desires, are unable without tremendous force of character to restrict themselves to a single channel long enough to profit by its trenching and deepening and wearing through. While the man of the twentieth century has use for instruments, like the radio and the phonograph and the telephone, which have no counterpart in other civilizations, the number of such commodities is in itself limited. No one is better off for having furniture that goes to pieces in a few years or, failing that happy means of creating a fresh demand, "goes out of style." No one is better dressed for having clothes so shabbily woven that they are worn out at the end of the season. On the contrary, such rapid consumption is a tax on production; and it tends to wipe out the gains the machine makes in that department. To the extent that people develop personal and esthetic interests, they are immune to trivial changes in style and they disdain to foster such low demands. Moreover, as Mr. J. A. Hobson has wisely pointed out, "if an undue amount of individuality be devoted to the production and consumption of food, clothing, etc., and the conscious, refined cultivation of these tastes, higher forms of individual expression in work and life will be neglected."

The second characteristic of vital wants is that they cannot be restricted to the bare elements of food enough to forestall starvation and clothing and shelter enough to satisfy convention and to ward off death by exposure. Life, from the very moment of birth on, requires for its fulfillment goods and services that are usually placed in the department of "luxuries." Song, story, music, painting, carving, idle play, drama—all these things lie outside the province of animal necessities: but they are not things which are to be included after the belly is satisfied: they are functions which must be included in human existence even to satisfy the belly, to say nothing of the emotional and intellectual and imaginative needs of man. To put these functions at a distance, to make them the goal of an acquisitive life, or to accept only so much of them as can be canalized into machine goods and sold at a profit—to do this is to misinterpret the nature of life as well as the possibilities of the machine.

The fact is that every vital standard has its own necessary luxuries; and the wage that does not include them is not a living wage, nor is the life made possible by bare subsistence a humane life. On the other hand, to set as a goal for universal economic effort, or at least to bait as a temptation, the imbecile standard of expenditure adopted by the rich and the powerful is merely to dangle a wooden carrot before the donkey; he cannot reach the carrot, and if he could, it still would not nourish him. A high scale of expense has no essential relation whatever to a high standard of living; and a plethora of machine-made goods has no essential relation, either, since one of the most essential elements of a good life—a pleasant and stimulating natural environment, both cultivated and primitive—is not a machine-made product. The notion that one implies the other is a figment of the business man's will-to-believe. As for what is called comfort, a good part of it, freedom from exertion, the extensive use of mechanical and personal service, leads in fact to an atrophy of function: the ideal is at best a valetudinarian one. The reliance for sensual pleasure upon inanimate objects—sofa pillows, upholstered furniture, sweetmeats, and soft textiles—was one of those devices whereby a bourgeois Puritanism, affecting to renounce the flesh and to castigate the body, merely acknowledged them in their most decadent forms, transferring attention from the animate bodies of men and women to objects that simulated them. The Renascence, which celebrated a vigorous sensual life, scarcely produced a comfortable chair in two hundred years: but one has only to look at the women painted by Veronese and Rubens to see how little such inorganic upholstery was needed.

As mechanical methods have become more productive, the notion has grown up that consumption should become more voracious. In back of this lies an anxiety lest the productivity of the machine create a glut in the market. The justification of labor-saving devices was not that they actually saved labor but that they increased consumption: whereas, plainly, labor-saving can take place only when the standard of consumption remains relatively stable, so that increases in conversion and in productive facility will be realized in the form of actual increments of leisure. Unfortunately, the capitalistic industrial system thrives by a denial of this condition. It thrives by stimulating wants rather than by limiting them and satisfying them. To acknowledge a goal of consummation would be to place a brake upon production and to lessen the opportunities for profit.

Technically speaking, changes in form and style are symptoms of immaturity; they mark a period of transition. The error of capitalism as a creed lies in the attempt to make this period of transition a permanent one. As soon as a contrivance reaches technical perfection, there is no excuse for replacement on the ground of increased efficiency: hence the devices of competitive waste, of shoddy workmanship, and of fashion must be resorted to. Wasteful consumption and shoddy craftmanship go hand in hand: so that if we value soundness and integrity and efficiency within the machine system, we must create a corresponding stability in consumption.

Speaking in the broadest terms this means that once the major wants of mankind are satisfied by the machine process, our factory system must be organized on a basis of regular annual replacement instead of progressive expansion—not on a basis of premature replacement through debauched workmanship, adulterated materials, and grossly stimulated caprice. "The case," as Mr. J. A. Hobson again puts it, "is a simple one. A mere increase in the variety of our material consumption relieves the strain imposed upon man by the limits of the material universe, for such variety enables him to utilize a larger proportion of the aggregate of matter. But in proportion as we add to mere variety a higher appreciation of those adaptations of matter which are due to human skill, which we call Art, we pass outside the limit of matter and are no longer the slaves of roods and acres and a law of diminishing returns." In other words: a genuine standard, once the vital physical wants are satisfied, tends to change the *plane* of consumption and therefore to limit, in a considerable degree, the extent of further mechanical enterprise.

But mark the vicious paradox of capitalist production. Although the factory system has been based on the doctrine of expanding wants and upon an expanding body of consumers, it has universally fallen short of supplying the normal wants of mankind. Horrified at the "utopian" notion of limited and normalized wants, and proudly proclaiming on the contrary that wants are insatiable, *capitalism has not come within miles of satisfying the most modest standard of normalized consumption.* Capitalism, with respect to the working mass of humanity, has been like a beggar that flaunts a hand covered with jewels, one or two of them genuine, whilst it shivers in rags and grabs at a crust of bread: the beggar may have money in the bank, too, but that does not improve his condition. This has been brought out clearly in every factual study that has been made of "advanced" industrial communities, from Charles Booth's classic survey of London to the thoroughly documented Pittsburgh survey: it has been re-enforced once more by Robert Lynd's study of the fairly representative community of "Middletown." What does one find? While the poorer inhabitants of Middletown often boast a motor car or a radio set, the houses they lived in during their period of putative prosperity often did not have even ordinary sanitary toilet facilities, while the state of the house and the general environment was, factually speaking, that of a slum.

When one says that the doctrine of increasing wants must be thrown overboard and the standard of consumption normalized, one does not in fact call for a contraction of our present industrial facilities. In many departments, on the contrary, we are urgently in need of an expansion of them. For the truth is that, despite all boasts of progress and mechanical achievement, despite all fears of surpluses and gluts, the mass of mankind, even in the countries that are technically the most advanced and financially the most prosperous, do not have—and apart from the agricultural population never have had—an adequate diet, proper facilities for hygiene, decent dwellings, sufficient means and opportunities for education and recreation. Indeed, in terms of vital norm a good part of these things have been equally lacking in the spurious standard of expenditure secured by the rich. In most great cities the urban dwellings of the upper classes, for example, are lacking in sunlight and open spaces, and are almost as inadequate as those of the very poor: so that, under a normalized standard of life, they would in many cases be healthier and happier than they are at present even though they would lack the illusion of success and power and distinction.

To normalize consumption is to erect a standard that no single class, whatever its expenditures, possesses today. But that standard cannot be expressed in terms of any arbitrary sum of money—the five thousand dollars per individual yearly suggested by Bellamy in the eighties, or the twenty thousand dollars suggested by a recent group of technocrats: for the point is that what five or twenty thousand dollars could purchase today for any single individual would not necessarily fulfill the more exacting vital requirements of this standard. And indeed, *the higher the vital standard, the less can it be expressed adequately in terms of money:* the more must it be expressed in terms of leisure, and health, and biological activity, and esthetic pleasure, and the more, therefore, will it tend to be expressed in terms of goods and environmental improvements that lie outside of machine production.

At the same time, the conception of a normalized consumption acknowledges the end of those princely capitalistic dreams of limitless incomes and privileges and sensuous vulgarities whose possession by the masters of society furnished endless vicarious gratification to their lackeys and imitators. Our goal is not *increased* consumption but a vital standard: less in the preparatory means, more in the ends, less in the mechanical apparatus, more in the organic fulfillment. When we have such a norm, our success in life will not be judged by the size of the rubbish heaps we have produced: it will be judged by the immaterial and non-consumable goods we have learned to enjoy, and by our biological fulfillment as lovers, mates, parents and by our personal fulfillment as thinking, feeling men and women. Distinction and individuality will reside in the personality, where it belongs, not in the size of the house we live in, in the expense of our trappings, or in the amount of labor we can arbitrarily command. Handsome bodies, fine minds, plain living, high thinking, keen perceptions, sensitive emotional responses, and a group life keyed to make these things possible and to enhance them—these are some of the objectives of a normalized standard.

While the animus that led to the expansion of the machine was narrowly utilitarian, the net result of such an economy is to create an antithetical stage, paralleled by the slave civilizations of old, endowed with an abundance of leisure. This leisure, if not vilely misused in the thoughtless production of more mechanical work, either through misplaced ingenuity or a vain consumptive ritual, may eventuate in a non-utilitarian form of society, dedicated more fully to play and thought and social intercourse and all those adventures and pursuits that make life more significant. The maximum of machinery and organization, the maximum of comforts and luxuries, the maximum of consumption, do not necessarily mean a maximum of life-efficiency or life-expression. The mistake consists in thinking that comfort, safety, absence of physical disease, a plethora of goods are the greatest blessings of civilization, and in believing that as they increase the evils of life will dissolve and disappear. But comfort and safety are not unconditioned goods; they are capable of defeating life just as thoroughly as hardship and uncertainty; and the notion that every other interest, art, friendship, love, parenthood, must be subordinated to the production of increasing amounts of comforts and luxuries is merely one of the superstitions of a money-bent utilitarian society.

By accepting this superstition the utilitarian has turned an elementary condition of existence, the necessity for providing a physical basis for life, into an end. As a result, our machine-dominated society is oriented solely to "things," and its members have every kind of possession except self-possession. No wonder that Thoreau observed that its members, even in an early and relatively innocent state of commerce and industry, led lives of quiet desperation. By putting business before every other manifestation of life, our mechanical and financial leaders have neglected the chief business of life: namely, growth, reproduction, development, expression. Paying infinite attention to the invention and perfection of incubators, they have forgotten the egg, and its reason for existence.

7: Basic Communism

A normalized mode of consumption is the basis of a rationalized mode of production. If one begins with production as an end in itself there is nothing within the machine system or the price system to guarantee a sufficient supply of vital goods. The capitalist economy attempted to avoid the necessity for erecting a real standard of life by relying upon the automatic operation of men's private interests, under the spell of the profit motive. All the necessary gains in production, along with a cheapening of the objects sold, were supposed to be an inevitable by-product of the business of buying cheap and selling where the demand was strongest and the supply scantest. The enlightened self-interest of individual buyers was the guarantee that the right things would be produced, in the right order, at the right time.

Lacking any standard for distributing income except on the basis of the gross labor performed and on the bare subsistence necessary to enable the worker to return each day to his job, this system never succeeded in its best days even on its own terms. The history of capitalism is the history of quantity production, over-expansion, greedy private over-capitalization on the basis of an increasing prospective income, the private appropriation of profits and dividends at the expense of the workers and the vast body of non-capitalist ultimate consumers—all followed, again and again, by a glut of unbought goods, a breakdown, bankruptcy, deflation, and the bitter starvation and depression of the working classes whose original inability to buy back the goods they had produced was always the major factor in this debacle.

This system is necessarily unworkable upon its own premises except perhaps under a pre-machine mode of production. For upon capitalist terms, the price of any commodity, roughly speaking, varies inversely as the quantity available at a given moment. This means that as production approaches infinity, the price of a single article must fall correspondingly toward zero. Up to a certain point, the fall in prices expands the market: beyond that point, the increase in real wealth for the community means a steady decrease in profits per unit for the manufacturer. If the prices are kept up without an expansion of real wages, an overplus occurs. If the price is lowered far enough, the manufacturer cannot, no matter how great his turnover, produce a sufficient margin of profit. Whereas mankind as a whole gains in wealth to the extent that the necessaries of life can, like the air, be had for the asking, the price system crashes into disaster long before this ideal point has been reached. Thus the gains in production under the price system must be diminished or cancelled out, as Veblen mordantly pointed out, by deliberate sabotage on the part of the financier and the business man. But this strategy has only a temporary effect: for the burden of debt, especially when recapitalized on the basis of a prospective expansion of the population and the market, ultimately outruns the curtailed productive capacities and subjects them to a load they cannot meet.

Now, the chief meaning of power conversion and mechanized production lies in the fact that they have created an economy of surplus —which is to say, an economy not adapted to the price system. As more and more work is transferred to automatic machines, the process of displacing workers from industry under this system is the equivalent of disfranchising them as consumers, since, unlike the holders of stock, bonds, and mortgages, they have no claim upon industry under capitalist conventions other than that resulting from their labor. It is useless to talk about temporary absorptions of labor by this or that industry: part of this absorption by the industries concerned with distribution only increases the overhead and the waste. And apart from this, under the system itself labor has lost both its bargaining power and its capacity to obtain subsistence: the existence of substitute industries sometimes postpones the individual but does not avert the collective day of reckoning. Lacking the power to buy the necessaries of life for themselves, the plight of the displaced workers reacts upon those who remain at work: presently the whole structure collapses, and even financiers and enterprisers and managers are sucked into the whirlpool their own cupidity, short-sightedness and folly have created. All this is a commonplace: but it rises, not as a result of some obscure uncontrollable law, like the existence of spots on the sun, but as the outcome of our failure to take advantage by adequate social provision of the new processes of mechanized production.

The problem presses for solution: but in one sense it has already been solved. For the better part of a thousand years, widows, orphans, and prudent sedentary people have been living at ease, buying food, drink, and shelter, without performing any work for the community. Their shares and their insurance payments constitute a first claim upon industry; and as long as there is any production of goods at all, and as long as the present legal conventions are maintained, they are sure of their means of existence. No capitalist talks about this system as one that demoralizes or undermines the self-respect of those who are so supported: indeed, the small incomes of the rentier classes have been an obvious help in the arts and sciences to their recipients: a Milton, a Shelley, a Darwin, a Ruskin existed by such grace; and one might even show, perhaps, that they had been more beneficial to society at large than the swollen fortunes of the more active capitalists. On the other hand, the small fixed income, though it sets at a distance the worst torments of economic distress, does not completely meet every economic requirement: so, in the case of the young and the ambitious, there is an incentive to productive and professional enterprise, even though the sting of starvation be absent.

The extension of this system to the community as a whole is what I mean by basic communism. In recent times, it was first seriously proposed by Edward Bellamy, in a somewhat arbitrary form, in his utopia, Looking Backward; and it has become plain during the last fifty years that an efficient mechanized system of production can be made serviceable to humanity at large in no other fashion. To make the worker's share in production the sole basis for his claim to a livelihood—as was done even by Marx in the labor theory of value he took over from Adam Smith—is, as power-production approaches perfection, to cut the ground from under his feet. In actuality, the claim to a livelihood rests upon the fact that, like the child in a family, one is a member of a community: the energy, the technical knowledge, the social heritage of a community belongs equally to every member of it, since in the large the individual contributions and differences are completely insignificant.

[*The classic name for such a universal system of distributing the essential means of life—as described by Plato and More long before Owen and Marx—is communism, and I have retained it here. But let me emphasize that this communism is necessarily post-Marxian, for the facts and values upon which it is based are no longer the paleotechnic ones upon which Marx founded his policies and programs. Hence communism, as used here, does not imply the particular nineteenth century ideology, the messianic absolutism, and the narrowly militarist tactics to which the official communist parties usually cling, nor does it imply a slavish imitation of the political methods and social institutions of Soviet Russia, however admirable soviet courage and discipline may be.*]

Differentiation and preference and special incentive should be taken into account in production and consumption only after the security and continuity of life itself is assured. Here and there we have established the beginnings of a basic communism in the provision of water and education and books. There is no rational reason for stopping short any point this side of a normal standard of consumption. Such a basis has no relation to individual capacities and virtues: a family of six requires roughly three times as much goods as a family of two, although there may be but one wage-earner in the first group and two in the second. We give at least a minimum of food and shelter and medical attention to criminals who have presumably behaved against the interests of society: why then should we deny it to the lazy and the stubborn? To assume that the great mass of mankind would belong to the latter category is to forget the positive pleasures of a fuller and richer life.

Moreover, under a scientific economy, the amount of grain, fruit, meat, milk, textiles, metals and raw materials, like the number of houses needed annually for replacement and for the increase of population, can be calculated in the gross in advance of production. It needs only the insurance of consumption to make the tables of production progressively more accurate. Once the standard was established, gains beyond those calculated would be bonuses for the whole community: such gains, instead of stopping the works, as they do now, would lubricate them, and so far from throwing the mechanism out of gear they would lighten the load for the whole community and increase the margin of time or energy available for the modes of life, rather than for the means.

To speak of a "planned economy," without such a basic standard of consumption and without the political means of making it prevail, is to mistake the monopolistic sabotage of large-scale capitalist industry for intelligent social control.

The foundations of this system of distribution already, I repeat, exist. Schools, libraries, hospitals, universities, museums, baths, lodging houses, gymnasia, are supported in every large center at the expense of the community as a whole. The police and the fire services, similarly, are provided on the basis of need instead of on the ability to pay: roads, canals, bridges, parks, playgrounds, and even—in Amsterdam—ferry services are similarly communized. Furthermore, in the most jejune and grudging form, a basic communism is in existence in countries that have unemployment and old-age insurance. But the latter measures are treated as means of salvage, rather than as a salutary positive mechanism for rationalizing the production and normalizing the consumptive standards of the whole community.

A basic communism, which implies the obligation to share in the work of the community up to the amount required to furnish the basis, does not mean the complete enclosure of every process and the complete satisfaction of every want in the system of planned production. Careful engineers have figured that the entire amount of work of the existing community could be carried on with less than twenty hours work per week for every existing worker: with complete rationalization all along the line, and with the elimination of duplications and parasitisms, probably less than twenty hours would suffice to produce a far greater quantity of goods than is produced at present. As it is, some 15 million industrial workers supply the needs of 120 million inhabitants of the United States. Limiting rationed production and communized consumption to basic requirements, the amount of compulsory labor would be even less. Under such provisions, technological unemployment would be a boon.

Basic communism would apply to the calculable economic needs of the community. It would touch those goods and services which can be standardized, weighed, measured, or about which a statistical computation can be made. Above such a standard the desire for leisure would compete with the desire for more goods: and here fashion, caprice, irrational choice, invention, special aims, would still perhaps have a part to play: for although all these elements have been grossly over-stimulated by capitalism, a residue of them would remain and would have to be provided for in any conceivable economic system. But under a basic communism, these special wants would not operate so as to disorganize production and paralyze distribution. With regard to the basic commodities there would be complete equality of income: and as consumption became normalized, the basic processes would care, in all probability, for a larger and larger part of the community's needs. On this basis—and so far as I can see on no other basis—can our gains in production and our growing displacement of human labor be realized in benefits for society at large. The alternative to basic communism is the toleration of chaos: either the closing down periodically of the productive plant and the destruction—quaintly called valorization—of essential goods, with shifty efforts at imperialist conquest to force open foreign markets; either that or a complete retreat from the machine into a sub-agriculture (subsistence farming) and a sub-industry (subsistence manufacture) which would be far lower in every way than what handicraft industry had provided in the eighteenth century. If we wish to retain the benefits of the machine, we can no longer afford to deny its chief social implication: namely, basic communism.

Not the least advantage of basic communism would be the fact that it would tend to put a brake upon industrial enterprise. But such a brake, instead of being in the form of capitalist sabotage, or in the shocking dislocation of a commercial crisis, would be a gradual lessening of the speed of individual parts and a gearing of the whole organization into a steady routine of productivity. Mr. J. A. Hobson has again put this matter with his usual insight and wisdom: "Industrial progress," he says, "would undoubtedly be slower under State-control, because the very object of such control is to divert a larger proportion of human genius and effort from these occupations [preparatory production] to apply them in producing higher forms of wealth. It is not, however, right to assume that progress in the industrial arts would cease under state-industry: such progress would be slower, and would itself partake of a routine character—a slow, continuous adjustment of the mechanism of production and distribution to the slowly changing needs of the community." However forbidding such a prospect looks to the enterpriser of the old order, humanly speaking it would represent a tremendous gain.

8: Socialize Creation!

During a great part of the history of mankind, from neolithic times onward, the highest achievements of the race in art and philosophy and literature and technics and science and religion were in the possession of a small caste of people. The technical means of multiplying these achievements were so cumbrous—the hieroglyphics of the Egyptians, the baked slabs of the Babylonian texts, even the hand-written letters on the papyrus or parchment of a later period—that the mastery of the implements of thought and expression was the

work of the better part of a lifetime. Those who had manual tasks
to perform were automatically excluded from most of the avenues of
creation outside their tasks, though they might eventually share in the
product created, at second or third hand. The life of the potter or
the smith, as Jesus ben Sirach pointed out with priggish but realistic
self-justification, unfitted him for the offices of the creative life.

This caste-monopoly was seriously disrupted during the Middle
Ages, partly because Christianity itself was in origin the religion of
the lowly and the downtrodden. Not merely was every human creature
a worthy subject of salvation, but within the monastery and the church
and the university there was a steady recruitment of novices and
students from every rank in society; and the powerful Benedictine
order, by making manual work itself one of the obligations of a disciplined life, broke down an ancient and crippling prejudice against
participation and experiment, as complementary to observation and
contemplation, in creative activity. Within the craft guilds the same
process took place in reverse direction: not merely did the journey-
man, in qualifying for his craft, get an opportunity to view critically
the arts and achievements of other cities, not merely was he encouraged to rise from the menial and mechanical operations of his
craft to such esthetic mastery as it offered, but in the performance
of the mysteries and the moralities the worker participated in the
esthetic and religious life of the whole community. Indeed the writer,
like Dante, could have a political status in this society only as the
member of a working guild.

The humanist movement, by placing an emphasis upon textual
scholarship and the dead languages to which this scholarship applied,
re-enforced the widened separation of classes under capitalism.
Unable to obtain the necessary preparatory training, the worker was
excluded from the higher culture of Europe: even the highest type
of eotechnic worker, the artist, and even one of the proudest figures
among these artists, Leonardo, felt obliged in his private notes to
defend himself against the assumption of the merely literate that
his interests in painting and science were somehow inferior.

Indifferent to the essential life of men as workers, this culture developed primarily as an instrument of caste-power, and only in a

feeble and secondary way for the benefit of mankind as a whole. From one end to the other some of the very best minds of the last three centuries, in the midst of their most vigorous creative efforts, have been apologizing for the injustices and perversions of their masters. Thorndike in his History of Science and Medicine in the Fifteenth Century notes the degradation that overcame thought when the free cities that Petrarch had known in his youth were enslaved by conquering armies: but the same fact is equally plain in Macchiavelli, Hobbes, Leibniz, Hegel; and this tendency of thought reached a certain climax in the misapplication of the Malthus-Darwin theory of the struggle for existence, to justify warfare, the nordic race, and the dominant position of the bourgeoisie.

But while the humanist side of this new culture was fostered on individualistic and caste lines, with a marked bias in favor of the possessing classes, science worked in an opposite direction. The very growth of scientific knowledge made it impossible to confine it, as a secret, to a small group, as astronomy was maintained in earlier civilizations. Not merely this, but science, by systematically utilizing the practical knowledge of artists and physicians in anatomy, of miners and metallurgists in chemistry, kept in touch with the working life of the community: was it not the predicament of vintners, brewers, and silkworm growers that roused Pasteur to his productive researches in bacteriology? Even when science was remote and by nature esoteric, it was not snobbish. Socialized in method, international in scope, impersonal in animus, performing some of its most hazardous and fruitful feats of thought by reason of its very divorce from immediate responsibility, the sciences have been slowly building up a grand cosmogony in which only one element is still lacking—the inclusion of the spectator and experimenter in the final picture.

Unfortunately, the dulling and depressing of the mind that inevitably followed from the division of labor and the bare routine of factory life, have opened an unnatural breach between science and technics and common practice and all the arts that lie outside the machine system. The workers themselves were thrown back upon the rubbish of earlier cultures, lingering in tradition and memory, and they clung to superstitious forms of religion which kept them in a state of emotional tutelage to the very forces that were exploiting them, or else they forfeited altogether the powerful emotional and moral stimulus that a genuine religion contributes to life. This applies likewise to the arts. The peasant and handworker of the Middle Age was the equal of the artists who carved and painted in his churches and his public halls: the highest art of that time was not too high for the common people, nor was there, apart from the affectations of court poesy, one kind of art for the few and another kind for the many. There were high and low levels in all this art: but the division was not marked by status or pecuniary condition.

During the last few centuries, however, popular means "vulgar" and "vulgar" means not simply the broadly human, but something inferior and crass and a little dehumanized. In short, instead of socializing the creative activities of society, we have socialized on a great scale only the low counterfeits of those activities: counterfeits that limit and stultify the mind. A Millet, a van Gogh, a Daumier, a Whitman, a Tolstoy naturally seek the working class for companionship: but they were actually kept alive and rewarded and appreciated chiefly by the very bourgeoisie whose manners they loathed and whose patronage they wished to escape. On the other hand, the experience of New England and New York between 1830 and 1860, when there was still to the westward a great sweep of unappropriated land, shows how fruitful an essentially classless society can be when it is nourished by the very occupations that a caste-culture disdains. It is no accident that the epic of Moby Dick was written by a common sailor, that Walden was written by a pencil-maker and surveyor, and that Leaves of Grass was written by a printer and carpenter. Only when it is possible to move freely from one aspect of experience and thought and action to another can the mind follow its complete trajectory. Division of labor and specialization, specialization between occupations, specialization in thought, can be justified only as temporary expedients: beyond that, as Kropotkin pointed out, lies the necessity of integrating labor and restoring its unity with life.

What we need, then, is the realization that the creative life, in all its manifestations, is necessarily a social product. It grows with the aid of traditions and techniques maintained and transmitted by society at large, and neither tradition nor product can remain the sole possession of the scientist or the artist or the philosopher, still less of the privileged groups that, under capitalist conventions, so largely support them. The addition to this heritage made by any individual, or even by any generation, is so small in comparison with the accumulated resources of the past that the great creative artists, like Goethe, are duly humble about their personal importance. To treat such activity as egoistic enjoyment or as property is merely to brand it as trivial: for the fact is that creative activity is finally the only important business of mankind, the chief justification and the most durable fruit of its sojourn on the planet. The essential task of all sound economic activity is to produce a state in which creation will be a common fact in all experience: in which no group will be denied, by reason of toil or deficient education, their share in the cultural life of the community, up to the limits of their personal capacity. Unless we socialize creation, unless we make production subservient to education, a mechanized system of production, however efficient, will only harden into a servile byzantine formality, enriched by bread and circuses.

9: Work for Automaton and Amateur

Not work, not production for its own sake or for the sake of ulterior profit, but production for the sake of life and work as the normal expression of a disciplined life, are the marks of a rational economic society. Such a society brings into existence choices and possibilities that scarcely existed so long as work was considered extraneous, and profit—or terror of starvation—was the chief impetus to labor.

The tendency of mechanization, from the seventeenth century on, has been to standardize the processes of work and to make them capable of machine operation. In power plants with automatic stokers, in advanced textile mills, in stamping factories, in various chemical works, the worker has scarcely any direct part in the process of production: he is, so to say, a machine-herd, attending to the welfare of a flock of machines which do the actual work: at best, he feeds them, oils them, mends them when they break down, while the work itself is as remote from his province as is the digestion which fattens the sheep looked after by the shepherd.

Such machine-tending often calls for alertness, non-repetitious movement, and general intelligence: in discussing neotechnics I pointed out that in industries that have advanced to this level the worker has recovered some of the freedom and self-direction that were frustrated in the more incomplete mechanical processes where the worker, instead of being general mechanic and overseer, is merely a substitute for the hand or eye that the machine has not yet developed. But in other processes, such as the straight line assemblage of the motor factory, for example, the individual worker is part of the process itself, and only a small fraction of him is engaged. Such labor is necessarily servile in character, and no amount of apology or psychological rationalization can make it otherwise: nor can the social necessity for the product mollify the process itself.

Our disregard for the quality of work itself, for work as a vital and educational process, is so habitual that it scarcely ever enters into our social demands. Yet it is plain that in the decision as to whether to build a bridge or a tunnel there is a human question that should outweigh the question of cheapness or mechanical feasability: namely, the number of lives that will be lost in the actual building or the advisability of condemning a certain number of men to spend their entire working days underground supervising tunnel traffic. As soon as our thought ceases to be automatically conditioned by the mine, such questions become important. Similarly the social choice between silk and rayon is not one that can be made simply on the different costs of production, or the difference in quality between the fibres themselves: there also remains, to be integrated in the decision, the question as to difference in working-pleasure between tending silkworms and assisting in rayon production. What the product contributes to the laborer is just as important as what the worker contributes to the product. A well-managed society might alter the process of motor car assemblage, at some loss of speed and cheapness, in order to produce a more interesting routine for the worker: similarly, it would either go to the expense of equipping dry-process cement making plants with dust removers—or replace the product itself with a less noxious substitute. When none of these alternatives was available, it would drastically reduce the demand itself to the lowest possible level.

Now, taken as a whole, including the preparatory processes of scientific investigation and mechanical design, to say nothing of the underlying political organization, industry is potentially a valuable instrument of education. This point, originally stressed by Karl Marx, was well put by Helen Marot when she said: "Industry offers opportunities for creative experience which is social in its processes as well as in its destination. The imaginative end of production does not terminate with the possession of an article; it does not center in the product or in the skill of this or that man, but in the development of commerce and technological processes and the evolution of world acquaintanceship and understanding. Modern machinery, the division of labor, the banking system, methods of communication, *make possible* real association. But they are real and possible only as the processes are open for the common participation, understanding, and judgment of those engaged in industrial enterprise; they are real and possible as the animus of industry changes from exploitation to a common and associated desire to create; they are real and possible as the individual character of industry gives way before the evolution of social effort."

Once the objective of industry is diverted from profit-making, private aggrandizement, crude exploitation, the unavoidable monotonies and restrictions will take a subordinate place, for the reason that the process will be humanized as a whole. This means that compensations for the repressive elements in the industrial routine will take place by adjustments within industry itself, instead of being permitted to heap up there, and to explode disastrously and anti-socially in other parts of society. To fancy that such a non-profit system is an impossibility is to forget that for thousands of years the mass of mankind knew no other system. The new economy of needs, replacing the capitalist economy of acquisition, will put the limited corporations and communities of the old economy on a broader and more intelligently socialized basis: but at bottom it will draw upon and canalize similar impulses. Despite all its chequered features and internal contradictions, this is to date perhaps the chief promise held out by Soviet Russia.

To the extent that industry must still employ human beings as machines, the hours of work must be reduced. We must determine the number of hours of blank routine per week that is within the limits of human tolerance, beyond which obvious deterioration of mind and spirit sets in. The very fact that purely repetitious work, without choices or variations, seems to agree with morons is enough to warn us of its dangers in relation to human beings of higher grade. But there remain occupations, machine-crafts as well as hand-crafts, which are interesting and absorbing in their own right, provided that they are not regimented too strictly in the interests of superficial efficiency. In the act of rationalizing and standardizing the methods of production, human engineering will have to weigh the social benefits of increased production with automatic machinery, with a lessened participation and satisfaction upon the part of the worker, against a lower level of production, with a larger opportunity for the worker. It is a shallow technicism to enforce the cheaper product at any price. Where the product is socially valuable and where the worker himself can be completely eliminated the answer will often, perhaps, favor automatism: but short of this state the decision cannot be lightly made. For no gain in production will justify the elimination of a humane species of work, unless other compensations in the way of work itself are at the same time provided. Money, goods, vacant leisure, cannot possibly make up for the loss of a life-work; although it is plain that money and goods, under our present abstract standards of success, are called upon often to do precisely this.

When we begin to rationalize industry organically, that is to say, with reference to the entire social situation, and with reference to the worker himself in all his biological capacities—not merely with reference to the crude labor product and an extraneous ideal of mechanical efficiency—the worker and his education and his environment become quite as important as the commodity he produces. We already acknowledge this principle on the negative side when we prohibit cheap lead glazes in pottery manufacture because the worker's health is undermined by their use: but it has a positive ap-

plication as well. Not merely should we prohibit work that is bad
for the health: we should promote work that is good for the health.
It is on these grounds that agriculture and our rural regions may
presently get back part of the population that was originally sucked
into the *villes tentaculaires* by the machine.

Labor itself, from spading a garden to mapping the stars, is one
of the permanent joys of life. A machine economy that permitted
mankind the inane and trivial leisure Mr. H. G. Wells once depicted
in The Time Machine, and that most city dwellers are condemned to
under capitalist society, particularly during periods of unemployment, would scarcely be worth the effort necessary to lubricate it:
such vacuity, such boredom, such debilitating lack of function do
not represent a gain of any kind. The chief benefit the rational use
of the machine promises is certainly not the elimination of work:
what it promises is something quite different—the elimination of
servile work or *slavery:* those types of work that deform the body,
cramp the mind, deaden the spirit. The exploitation of machines is
the alternative to that exploitation of degraded men that was practiced throughout antiquity and that was challenged on a large scale,
for the first time, in the power economy evolved in the eotechnic
phase.

By the completion of our machine organization, we can recover
for work the inherent values which it was robbed of by the pecuniary
aims and class animosities of capitalist production. The worker,
properly extruded from mechanical production as slave, comes back
as director: if his instincts of workmanship are still unsatisfied by
these managerial tasks, he has by reason of the power and leisure
he now potentially commands a new status within production as an
amateur. The gain in freedom here is a direct compensation for the
pressure and duress, for the impersonality, the anonymity, the collective unity of machine production.

Beyond the basic needs of production, beyond a normalized—and
therefore moralized—standard of life, beyond the essential communism in consumption I have posited, there lie wants which the
individual or the group has no right to demand from society at large,
and which, in turn, society has no need to curtail or arbitrarily re-

press in the individual, so long as the motive of exploitation is removed. These wants may be satisfied by direct effort. To weave or knit clothes by hand, to produce a necessary piece of furniture, to experimentally build an airplane on lines that have not won official approval—these are samples of occupations open to the individual, the household, the small working group, apart from the regular channels of production. Similarly, while the great staples in agriculture, like wheat, corn, hogs, beef, will possibly tend to be the work of large cooperatives, green vegetables and flowers may be raised by individuals on a scale impossible so long as land was privately appropriated and the mass of industrial mankind was packed together in solid areas of house and pavement.

As our basic production becomes more impersonal and routinized, our subsidiary production may well become more personal, more experimental, and more individualized. This could not happen under the older régime of handicraft: it was a development not possible before the neotechnic improvements of the machine with electricity as a source of power. For the acquisition of skill necessary for efficient production on a handicraft basis was a tedious process, and the slow tempo of handicraft in the essential occupations did not give a sufficient margin of time for achievement along other lines. Or rather, the margin was achieved by the subordination of the working class and the elevation of a small leisure class: the worker and the amateur represented two different strata. With electric power a small machine shop may have all the essential devices and machine tools— apart from specialized automatic machines—that only a large plant could have afforded a century ago: so the worker can regain, even within the machine occupations, most of the pleasure that the machine itself, by its increasing automatism, has been taking away from him. Such workshops connected with schools should be part of the public equipment of every community.

The work of the amateur, then, is a necessary corrective to the impersonality, the standardization, the wholesale methods and products of automatic production. But it is likewise an indispensable educational preparation for the machine process itself. All the great advances in machines have been on the basis of the handicraft operations or scientific thought—itself aided and corrected by small-scale manual operations called experiments. As "technological tenuousness" increases, the diffusion of handicraft knowledge and skill as a mode of education is necessary, both as a safety device and as a means to further insight, discovery, and invention. For the machine cannot know more or do more than the human eye or hand or mind that designs or operates it. Given knowledge of the essential operations, one could reconstruct every machine in the world. But let that knowledge be cut off for so much as a single generation, and all the complicated derivatives would be so much junk. If parts broke and rusted without being immediately replaced, the whole fabric would be in ruins. And there is still a further reason to give an important position to the hand-crafts and machine-crafts, as subsidiary forms of production, run on a domestic scale. For both safety and flexibility in all forms of industrial production it is important that we learn to travel light. Our specialized automatic machines, precisely because of their high degree of specialization, lack adaptability to new forms of production: a change in demand, a change in pattern, leads to the wholesale scrapping of very expensive equipment. Wherever demand for products is of an uncertain or variable nature, it is an economy in the long run to use non-specialized machines: this decreases the burden of wasted effort and idle machinery. What is true of the machine is equally true of the worker: instead of a high degree of specialized skill, an all-round competence is better preparation for breaking through stale routines and for facing emergencies.

It is the basic skills, the basic manual operations, the basic discoveries, the basic formulas which must be transmitted from generation to generation. To maintain the superstructure whilst we let the foundations moulder away is to endanger not alone the existence of our complicated civilization but its further development and refinement. For critical changes and adaptations in machines, as in organisms, come not from the differentiated and specialized stock, but from the relatively undifferentiated common ancestor: it was the foot-treadle that served Watt's need for transmitting power in a steam engine. Automatic machines may conquer an ever-larger province in basic production: but it must be balanced by the hand-crafts and the machine-crafts for education, recreation, and experiment. Without the second, automatism would ultimately be a blight on society, and its further existence would be imperilled.

10: Political Control

Plan and order are latent in all modern industrial processes, in the working drawing, in the preliminary calculations, in the organization chart, in the time-schedule, in the graphs that keep track of production day by day, and even hour by hour, as in a power plant. This graphic and ordered procedure, originating in the separate techniques of the civil engineer, the architect, the mechanical engineer, the forester, and other types of technician, is particularly evident in the neotechnic industries. (See, for example, the elaborate economic and social surveys of the Bell Telephone Company, in preparation for establishing or extending services.) What is still lacking is the transference of these techniques from industry to the social order at large. The order so far established is too local to be socially effective on a great scale, and apart from Soviet Russia the social apparatus is either antiquated, as in the "democratic" countries, or renovated in archaic forms, as in the even more backward Fascist countries. In short, our political organization is either paleotechnic or pre-technic. Hence the hiatus between the mechanical achievements and the social results. We have now to work out the details of a new political and social order, radically different by reason of the knowledge that is already at our command from any that now exists. And to the extent that this order is the product of scientific thought and humanistic imagination, it will leave a place for irrational and instinctive and traditional elements in society which were flouted, to their own ultimate peril, by the narrow forms of rationalism that prevailed during the past century.

The transformation of the worker's status in industry can come about only through a three-fold system of control: the functional political organization of industry from within, the organization of the consumers as active and self-regulating groups, giving rational expression to collective demands, and the organization of industries as units within the political framework of cooperating states.

The internal organization implies the transformation of the trade union from a bargaining organization, seeking special privileges apart from the industry or the working class as a whole, into a producing organization, concerned with establishing a standard of production, a humane system of management, and a collective discipline which will include every member, from such unskilled workers who may enter as apprentices up to the administrators and engineers. In the nineteenth century the mass of workers, cowed, uneducated, unskilled in cooperation, were only too willing to permit the capitalists to retain the responsibilities for financial management and production: their unions sought for the most part merely to obtain for the worker a greater share of the income, and somewhat more favorable conditions of labor.

The enterpriser, in turn, looked upon the management of his industry as a god-given right of ownership: to hire and fire, to stop and start, to build and destroy were special rights which neither the worker nor the government could encroach upon. The development of laws restricting the hours of labor and establishing minimum sanitary conditions, the development of public control of important public utilities, the growth of cartels and semi-monopolistie trade organizations under government supervision, have broken down this self-sufficiency of the manufacturer. But these measures, though struggled for by the worker, have done little to increase his dynamic participation in the management of industry itself. While here and there moves have been made toward a more positive integration of labor, as in the Baltimore and Ohio Railroad machine shops and in certain sections of the Garment Industry in America, for the most part the worker has no responsibility beyond his detailed job.

Until the worker emerges from a state of spiritless dependence there can be no large gain either in collective efficiency or in social direction: by its nature autonomy is something that cannot be handed from above. For the functional organization of industry there must be collective discipline, collective efficiency, above all collective responsibility: along with this must go a deliberate effort to produce engineering and scientific and managerial talent from within the ranks of the workers themselves, in addition to enlisting the services of more socialized members of this group, who are already spiritually developed beyond the lures and opportunities of the financial system to which they are attached. Without growth within the factory of effective units for work, the position of the worker, no matter what the ostensible nature of the political system, must remain a precarious and servile one; for the increase of mechanization vitiates his bargaining power, the increasing ranks of the unemployed tend automatically to beat down his wages, and the periodical disorganization of industry cancels out any small gains he may momentarily make. Plainly, such control, such autonomy, will not be achieved without a struggle—internal struggle for training and knowledge, and an external struggle against the weapons and the instruments handed down from the past. In the long run this struggle involves a fight not only against a sessile administrative bureaucracy within the trade unions themselves; more importantly, it involves an outright battle with the guardians of capitalism. Fortunately, the moral bankruptcy of the capitalist system is an opportunity as well as an obstacle: a decayed institution, though more dangerous to live with than a sound one, is easier to remove. The victory over the possessing classes is not the goal of this struggle: that is but a necessary incident in the effort to achieve a solidly integrated and socialized basis for industry. The struggle for power is a futile one, no matter who is victorious, unless it is directed by the will-to-function. Fascism has effaced the workers' attempts to overwhelm the capitalist system in Italy and Germany because ultimately the workers had no plan for carrying the fight beyond the stage of fighting.

The point to remember, however, is that the power needed to operate and to transform our modern technics is something other than physical force. The whole organization of modern industry is a complicated one, dependent upon a host of professionalized skills that link into each other, dependent likewise upon the faith and good will of those interchanging services, data, and calculations. Unless there is an inner coherence here, no amount of supervision will ensure against knavery and non-cooperation. This society cannot be run by brute force or by servile truculent skill backed by brute force: in the long run such habits of action are self-defeating. The principle

of functional autonomy and functional responsibility must be observed at every stage of the process, and the contrary principle of
class domination, based upon a privileged status—whether that class
be aristocratic or proletarian—is technically and socially inefficient.
Moreover, technics and science demand autonomy and self-control,
that is, freedom, in the realm of thought. The attempt to limit this
functional autonomy by the erection of special dogmas, as the
Christians limited it in the early days of Christianity, will cause a
fall into cruder methods of thinking, inimical to the essential basis
of both technics and modern civilization.

As industry advances in mechanization, a greater weight of political power must develop outside it than was necessary in the past. To
counterbalance the remote control and the tendency to continue along
the established grooves of industrial effort there must arise a collective organization of consumers for the sake of controlling the
kind and quantity and distribution of the product itself. In addition
to the negative check to which all industry is subject, the struggle for
existence between competing commodities, there must be a positive
mode of regulation which will ensure the production of desirable
types of commodities. Without such organization even our semi-com-
petitive commercial regime is slow in adapting itself to demand: at
the very moment that it changes, from month to month and year to
year, the superficial styles of its products, it resists the introduction
of fresh ideas, as the American furniture industry for long and stub-
bornly resisted the introduction of non-period furniture. Under a
more stable noncompetitive organization of industry, consumers'
groups for formulating and imposing demands will be even more
important for rational production: without such groups any central
agency for determining lines of production and quotas must necessarily be arbitrary and inefficient. Meanwhile the erection of scientific scales of performance and material quality—so that goods will
be sold on the basis of actual value and service, rather than on the
basis of clever packaging and astute advertising—is a natural corol-
lary on the consumer's side to the rationalization of industry. The
failure to use the existing laboratories for determining such standards—like the National Bureau of Standards in the United States—

for the benefit of the entire body of consumers is one of the most impudent miscarriages of knowledge under the capitalist system.

The third necessary element of political control lies in the possession of land, capital, credit, and machines. In America, which has reached an advanced stage of both mechanical improvement and financial organization, almost fifty per cent of the capital invested in industry, and something over forty per cent of the income of the nation, is concentrated in two hundred corporations. These corporations are so huge and have their capital in so many shares, that in no one of them does any particular person control by ownership more than five per cent of the capital invested. In other words, administration and ownership, which had a natural affiliation in small-scale enterprise, are now almost completely divorced in the major industries. (This condition was astutely used during the last two decades, by the bankers and administrators of American industry, for example, to appropriate for their private advantage a lion's share of the income, by a process of systematic pillage through recapitalization and bonuses.) Since the present shareholders of industry have already been dispossessed by the machinations of capitalism itself, there would be no serious jar if the system were put on a rational basis, by placing the banking functions directly under the state, and collecting capital directly out of the earnings of industry instead of permitting it to be routed in a roundabout fashion through acquisitive individuals, whose knowledge of the community's needs is empirical and unscientific and whose public interest is vitiated by private concerns—if not by outright anti-social animus. Such a change in the financial structure of our major instruments of production is a necessary prelude to humanizing the machine. Naturally, this means a revolution: whether it shall be humane or bloody, whether it shall be intelligent or brutal, whether it shall be accomplished smoothly, or with a series of violent shocks and jerks and catastrophes, depends to a large extent upon the quality of mind and the state of morals that exists among the present directors of industry and their opponents.

Now, the necessary impulses toward such a change are already apparent within the bankrupt structure of capitalist society: during its seizures of paralysis, it openly begs for the state to come in and rescue it and put it once more on its feet. Once the wolf is driven away, capitalism becomes brave again: but at scarcely any point during the last century has it been able to live without the help of state subsidies, state privileges, state tariffs, to say nothing of the aid of the state in subduing and regimenting the workers when the two groups have broken out into open warfare. Laissez-faire is in fact advocated and preached by capitalism only during those rare moments when it is doing well without the help of the state: but in its imperialist phase, laissez-faire is the last thing that capitalism desires. What it means by that slogan is not Hands off Industry—but Hands off Profits! In concluding his monumental survey of Capitalism Sombart looks upon 1914 as a turning-point for capitalism itself. The signs of the change are the impregnation of capitalistic modes of existence with normative ideas: the displacement of the struggle for profit as the sole condition of orientation in industrial relations, the undermining of private competition through the principle of understandings, and the constitutional organization of industrial enterprise. These processes, which have actually begun under capitalism, have only to be pushed to their logical conclusions to carry us beyond the capitalist order. Rationalization, standardization, and above all, rationed production and consumption, on the scale necessary to bring up to a vital norm the consumptive level of the whole community—these things are impossible on a sufficient scale without a socialized political control of the entire process.

If such a control cannot be instituted with the cooperation and intelligent aid of the existing administrators of industry, it must be achieved by overthrowing them and displacing them. The application of new norms of consumption, as in the housing of workers, has during the last thirty years won the passive support, sometimes subsidies drawn from taxation, of the existing governments of Europe, from conservative London to communistically bent Moscow. But such communities, while they have challenged and supplemented capitalist enterprise, are merely indications of the way in which the wind is blowing. Before we can replan and reorder our entire environment,

on a scale commensurate with our human needs, the moral and legal
and political basis of our productive system will have to be sharply
revised. Unless such a revision takes place, capitalism itself will be
eliminated by internal rot: lethal struggles will take place between
states seeking to save themselves by imperialist conquest, as they will
take place between classes within the state, jockeying for a power
which will take the form of brute force just to the extent that society's
grip on the productive mechanism itself is weakened.

11: The Diminution of the Machine

Most of the current fantasies of the future, which have been suggested by the triumph of the machine, are based upon the notion that
our mechanical environment will become more pervasive and oppressive. Within the past generation, this belief seemed justified: Mr.
H. G. Wells's earlier tales of The War of the Worlds and When the
Sleeper Wakes, predicted horrors, great and little, from gigantic
aerial combats to the blatant advertisement of salvation by go-getting
Protestant churches—horrors that were realized almost before the
words had left his mouth.

The belief in the greater dominance of mechanism has been re-
enforced by a vulgar error in statistical interpretation: the belief that
curves generated by a past historic complex will continue without
modification into the future. Not merely do the people who hold
these views imply that society is immune to qualitative changes: they
imply that it exhibits uniform direction, uniform motion, and even
uniform acceleration—a fact which holds only for simple events in
society and for very minor spans of time. The fact is that social predictions that are based upon past experience are always retrospective: they do not touch the real future. That such predictions have
a way of justifying themselves from time to time is due to another
fact: namely that in what Professor John Dewey calls judgments
of practice the hypothesis itself becomes one of the determining
elements in the working out of events: to the extent that it is seized
and acted upon it weights events in its favor. The doctrine of
mechanical progress doubtless had such a rôle in the nineteenth
century.

What reason is there to believe that the machine will continue to multiply indefinitely at the rate that characterized the past, and that it will take over even more territory than it has already conquered? While the inertia of society is great, the facts of the matter lend themselves to a different interpretation. The rate of growth in all the older branches of machine production has in fact been going down steadily: Mr. Bassett Jones even holds that this is generally true of all industry since 1910. In those departments of mechanical industry that were well-established by 1870, like the railroad and the textile mill, this slowing down applies likewise to the critical inventions. Have not the conditions that forced and speeded the earlier growth— namely, the territorial expansion of Western Civilization and the tremendous increase in population—been diminishing since that point?

Certain machines, moreover, have already reached the limit of their development: certain areas of scientific investigation are already completed. The printing press, for example, reached a high pitch of perfection within a century after its invention: a whole succession of later inventions, from the rotary press to the linotype and monotype machines, while they have increased the pace of production, have not improved the original product: the finest page that can be produced today is no finer than the work of the sixteenth century printers. The water turbine is now ninety per cent efficient; we cannot, on any count, add more than ten per cent to its efficiency. Telephone transmission is practically perfect, even over long distances; the best the engineers can now do is to multiply the capacity of the wires and to extend the inter-linkages. Distant speech and vision cannot be transmitted faster than they are transmitted today by electricity: what gains we can make are in cheapness and ubiquity. In short: there are bounds to mechanical progress within the nature of the physical world itself. It is only by ignoring these limiting conditions that a belief in the automatic and inevitable and limitless expansion of the machine can be retained.

And apart from any wavering of interest in the machine, a general increase in verified knowledge in other departments than the physical sciences already threatens a large curtailment of mechanical practices and instruments. It is not a mystic withdrawal from the practical concerns of the world that challenges the machine so much as a more comprehensive knowledge of phenomena to which our mechanic contrivances were only partial and ineffective responses. Just as, within the domain of engineering itself, there has been a growing tendency toward refinement and efficiency through a nicer inter-relation of parts, so in the environment at large the province of the machine has begun to shrink. When we think and act in terms of an organic whole, rather than in terms of abstractions, when we are concerned with life in its full manifestation, rather than with the fragment of it that seeks physical domination and that projects itself in purely mechanical systems, we will no longer require from the machine alone what we should demand through a many-sided adjustment of every other aspect of life. A finer knowledge of physiology reduces the number of drugs and nostrums in which the physician places confidence: it also decreases the number and scope of surgical operations—those exquisite triumphs of machine-technics!—so that although refinements in technique have increased the number of potential operations that can be resorted to, competent physicians are tempted to exhaust the resources of nature before utilizing a mechanical shortcut. In general, the classic methods of Hippocrates have begun to displace, with a new certitude of conviction, both the silly potions prescribed in Molière's Imaginary Invalid and the barbarous intervention of Mr. Surgeon Cuticle. Similarly, a sounder notion of the human body has relegated to the scrapheap most of the weight-lifting apparatus of late Victorian gymnastics. The habit of doing without hats and petticoats and corsets has, in the past decade, thrown whole industries into limbo: a similar fate, through the more decent attitude toward the naked human body, threatens the bathing suit industry. Finally, with a great part of the utilities, like railroads, power lines, docks, port facilities, automobiles, concrete roads which we constructed so busily during the last hundred years, we are now on a basis where repair and replacement are all that is required. As our production becomes more rationalized, and as population shifts and regroups in better relationship to industry and recreation, new communities designed to the human scale are being constructed. This movement which has been taking place in Europe during the last generation is

a result of pioneering work done over a century from Robert Owen
to Ebenezer Howard. As these new communities are built up the
need for the extravagant mechanical devices like subways, which
were built in response to the disorganization and speculative chaos of
the megalopolis, will disappear.

In a word, *as social life becomes mature, the social unemployment
of machines will become as marked as the present technological unemployment of men.* Just as the ingenious and complicated mechanisms for inflicting death used by armies and navies are marks of international anarchy and painful collective psychoses, so are many of our
present machines the reflexes of poverty, ignorance, disorder. The
machine, so far from being a sign in our present civilization of human power and order, is often an indication of ineptitude and social
paralysis. Any appreciable improvement in education and culture
will reduce the amount of machinery devoted to multiplying the
spurious mechanical substitutes for knowledge and experience now
provided through the channels of the motion picture, the tabloid newspaper, the radio, and the printed book. So, too, any appreciable improvement in the physical apparatus of life, through better nutrition,
more healthful housing, sounder forms of recreation, greater opportunities for the natural enjoyments of life, will decrease the part
played by mechanical apparatus in salvaging wrecked bodies and
broken minds. Any appreciable gain in personal harmony and balance will be recorded in a decreased demand for compensatory
goods and services. The passive dependence upon the machine that
has .characterized such large sections of the Western World in the
past was in reality an abdication of life. Once we cultivate the arts
of life directly, the proportion occupied by mechanical routine and
by mechanical instruments will again diminish.

Our mechanical civilization, contrary to the assumption of those
who worship its external power the better to conceal their own feeling
of impotence, is not an absolute. All its mechanisms are dependent
upon human aims and desires: many of them flourish in direct proportion to our failure to achieve rational social cooperation and integrated personalities. Hence we do not have to renounce the machine
completely and go back to handicraft in order to abolish a good deal

of useless machinery and burdensome routine: we merely have to use imagination and intelligence and social discipline in our traffic with the machine itself. In the last century or two of social disruption, we were tempted by an excess of faith in the machine to do everything by means of it. We were like a child left alone with a paint brush who applies it impartially to unpainted wood, to varnished furniture, to the tablecloth, to his toys, and to his own face. When, with increased knowledge and judgment, we discover that some of these uses are inappropriate, that others are redundant, that others are inefficient substitutes for a more vital adjustment, we will contract the machine to those areas in which it serves directly as an instrument of human purpose. The last, it is plain, is a large area: but it is probably smaller than that now occupied by the machine. One of the uses of this period of indiscriminate mechanical experiment was to disclose unsuspected points of weakness in society itself. Like an old-fashioned menial, the arrogance of the machine grew in proportion to its master's feebleness and folly. With a change in ideals from material conquest, wealth, and power to life, culture, and expression, the machine like the menial with a new and more confident master, will fall back into its proper place: our servant, not our tyrant.

Quantitatively, then, we shall probably be less concerned with production in future than we were forced to be during the period of rapid expansion that lies behind us. So, too, we shall probably use fewer mechanical instruments than we do at present, although we shall have a far greater range to select from, and shall have more skillfully designed, more finely calibrated, more economical and reliable contrivances than we now possess. The machines of the future, if our present technics continues, will surpass those in use at present as the Parthenon surpassed a neolithic wood-hut: the transformation will be both toward durability and to refinement of forms. The dissociation of production from the acquisitive life will favor technical conservatism on a high level rather than a flashy experimentalism on a low level.

But this change will be accompanied by a qualitative change in interest, too: in general a change from mechanical interest to vital and psychal and social interests. This potential change in interest is generally ignored in predictions about the future of the machine. Yet once its importance is grasped it plainly alters every purely quantitative prediction that is based upon the assumption that the interests which for three centuries have operated chiefly within a mechanical framework will continue to remain forever within that framework. On the contrary, proceeding under the surface in the work of poets and painters and biological scientists, in a Goethe, a Whitman, a von Mueller, a Darwin, a Bernard, there has been a steady shift in attention from the mechanical to the vital and the social: more and more, adventure and exhilarating effort will lie here, rather than within the already partly exhausted field of the machine.

Such a shift will change the incidence of the machine and profoundly alter its relative position in the whole complex of human thought and activity. Shaw, in his Back to Methuselah, put such a change in a remote future; and risky though prophecy of this nature be, it seems to me that it is probably already insidiously at work. That such a movement could not take place, certainly not in science and its technical applications, without a long preparation in the inorganic realm is now fairly obvious: it was the relative simplicity of the original mechanical abstractions that enabled us to develop the technique and the confidence to approach more complicated phenomena. But while this movement toward the organic owes a heavy debt to the machine, it will not leave its parent in undisputed possession of the field. In the very act of enlarging its dominion over human thought and practice, the machine has proved to a great degree self-eliminating: its perfection involves in some degree its disappearance —as a communal water-system, once built, involves less daily attention and less expense on annual replacements than would a hundred thousand domestic wells and pumps. This fact is fortunate for the race. It will do away with the necessity, which Samuel Butler satirically pictured in Erewhon, for forcefully extirpating the dangerous troglodytes of the earlier mechanical age. The old machines will in part die out, as the great saurians died out, to be replaced by smaller, faster, brainer, and more adaptable organisms, adapted not to the mine, the battlefield and the factory, but to the positive environment of life.

12: Toward a Dynamic Equilibrium

The chief justification of the gigantic changes that took place during the nineteenth century was the fact of change itself. No matter what happened to human lives and social relations, people looked upon each new invention as a happy step forward toward further inventions, and society went on blindly like a caterpillar tractor, laying down its new road in the very act of lifting up the old one. The machine was supposed to abolish the limits of movement and of growth: machines were to become bigger: engines were to become more powerful: speeds were to become faster: mass production was to multiply more vastly: the population itself was to keep on increasing indefinitely until it finally outran the food supply or exhausted the soil of nitrogen. So went the nineteenth century myth.

Today, the notion of progress in a single line without goal or limit seems perhaps the most parochial notion of a very parochial century. Limits in thought and action, norms of growth and development, are now as present in our consciousness as they were absent to the contemporaries of Herbert Spencer. In our technics, countless improvements of course remain to be made, and there are doubtless numerous fresh fields still to be opened: but even in the realm of pure mechanical achievement we are already within sight of natural limits, not imposed by human timidity or lack of resources or immature technics, but by the very nature of the elements with which we work. The period of exploration and unsystematic, sporadic advance, which seemed to the nineteenth century to embody the essential characteristics of the new economy, is rapidly coming to an end. We are now faced with the period of consolidation and systematic assimilation. Western Civilization as a whole, in other words, is in the condition that new pioneering countries like the United States found themselves in, once all their free lands had been taken up and their main lines of transportation and communication laid out: it must now begin to settle down and make the most of what it has. Our machine system is beginning to approach a state of internal equilibrium. Dynamic equilibrium, not indefinite progress, is the mark of the opening age: balance, not rapid one-sided advance: conservation, not reckless pillage. The parallel between neolithic and neotechnic times holds even here: for the main advances which were consolidated in neolithic times remained stable, with minor variations within the pattern, for between 2500 and 3500 years. Once we have generally reached a new technical plateau we may remain on that level with very minor ups and down for thousands of years. What are the implications of this approaching equilibrium?

First: equilibrium in the environment. This means first the restoration of the balance between man and nature. The conservation and restoration of soils, the re-growth wherever this is expedient and possible, of the forest cover to provide shelter for wild life and to maintain man's primitive background as a source of recreation, whose importance increases in proportion to the refinement of his cultural heritage. The use of tree crops where possible as substitutes for annuals, and the reliance upon kinetic energy—sun, falling water, wind—instead of upon limited capital supplies. The conservation of minerals and metals: the larger use of scrap metals. The conservation of the environment itself as a resource, and the fitting of human needs into the pattern formed by the region as a whole: hence the progressive restoration out of such unbalanced regions as the over-urbanized metropolitan areas of London and New York. Is it necessary to point out that all this marks the approaching end of the miner's economy? Not mine and move, but stay and cultivate are the watchwords of the new order. Is it also necessary to emphasize that with respect to our use of metals, the conservative use of the existing supply will lower the importance of the mine in relation to other parts of the natural environment?

Second: equilibrium in industry and agriculture. This has rapidly been taking place during the last two generations in the migration of modern technics from England to America and to the rest of Europe, and from all these countries in turn to Africa and Asia. No one center is any longer the home of modern industry or its sole focal point: the finest work in rapid motion picture photography has been done in Japan, and the most astounding instrument of cheap mass production is the Bata Shoe Factories of Czechoslovakia. The more or less uniform distribution of mechanical industry over every portion of the planet tends to produce a balanced industrial life in every region: ultimately a state of balance over the earth itself. A similar advance remains to be worked out more largely for agriculture. With the decentralization of population into new centers, encouraged by motor and aerial transportation and by giant power, and with the application of scientific methods to the culture of soils and the processes of agriculture, as so admirably practiced today in Belgium and Holland, there is a tendency to equalize advantage between agricultural regions. With economic regionalism the area of market gardening and mixed farming—already favored by the scientific transformation of our diet—will widen again, and specialized farming for world export will tend to diminish except where, as in industry, some region produces specialties that cannot easily be duplicated.

Once the regional balance between industry and agriculture is worked out in detail, production in both departments will be on a more stable basis. This stability is the technical side of the normalization of consumption with which I have already dealt. Since at bottom the profit-motive arose out of and was furthered by uncertainty and speculation, whatever stability specialized capitalism had in the past rested on its capacity for promoting change, and taking advantage of it. Its safety rested upon its progressive tendency to revolutionize the means of production, promote new shifts in population, and take advantage of the speculative disorder. The equilibrium of capitalism, in other words, was the equilibrium of chaos. Per contra, the forces that work toward a normalization of consumption, toward a planned and rationed production, toward a conservation of resources, toward a planned distribution of population are in sharp opposition by reason of their essential technics to the methods of the past: hence an inherent conflict between this technology and the dominant capitalist methods of exploitation. As we approach an industrial and agricultural equilibrium part of the *raison d'être* of capitalism itself will vanish.

Third: equilibrium in population. There are parts of the Western World in which there is a practical balance between the number of births and deaths: most of these countries, France, Great Britain, the

United States, the Scandinavian countries, are in a relatively high state of technical and cultural development. The blind animal pressure of births, responsible for so many of the worst features of nineteenth century development, is now characteristic in the main of backward countries, countries in a state of political or technical inferiority. If equilibrium takes place here during the next century one may look forward to a rational re-settlement of the entire planet into the regions most favorable to human habitation: an era of deliberate recolonization will take the place of those obstreperous and futile conquests which began with the explorations of the Spaniards and the Portuguese in the sixteenth century and which have continued without any essential change down to the most recent raids of the Japanese. Such an internal re-settlement is already taking place in many countries: the movement of industries into Southern England, the development of the French Alps, the settlement of new farmers in Palestine and Siberia, are first steps toward achieving a state of equilibrium. The balancing off of the birth-rate and death-rate, and the balancing off of rural and urban environments—with the wholesale wiping out of the blighted industrial areas inherited from the past—are all part of a single integration.

This state of balance and equilibrium—regional, industrial, agricultural, communal—will work a further change within the domain of the machine itself: a change of tempo. The temporary fact of increasing acceleration, which seemed so notable to Henry Adams when he surveyed the progress from twelfth century unity to twentieth century multiplicity, the fact which was later accompanied by a belief in change and speed for their own sake—will no longer characterize our society. It is not the absolute speed assumed by any part of the machine system that indicates efficiency: what is important is the relative speed of the various parts with a view to the ends to be accomplished: namely, the maintenance and development of human life. Efficiency, even on the technical level alone, means a gearing together of the various parts so that they may deliver the correct and the predictable amounts of power, goods, services, utilities. To achieve this efficiency, it may be necessary to lower the tempo rather than to increase it in this or that department; and as larger portions of our days go to leisure and smaller portions to work, as our thinking becomes synthetic and related, instead of abstract and pragmatic, as we turn to the cultivation of the whole personality instead of centering upon the power elements alone—as all these things come about we may look forward to a slowing of the tempo throughout our lives, even as we may look forward to a lessening of the number of unnecessary external stimuli. Mr. H. G. Wells has characterized the approaching period as the Era of Rebuilding. No part of our life, our thought, or our environment can escape that necessity and that obligation.

The problem of tempo: the problem of equilibrium: the problem of organic balance: in back of them all the problem of human satisfaction and cultural achievement—these have now become the critical and all-important problems of modern civilization. To face these problems, to evolve appropriate social goals and to invent appropriate social and political instruments for an active attack upon them, and finally to carry them into action: here are new outlets for social intelligence, social energy, social good will.

13: Summary and Prospect

We have studied the origins, the advances, the triumphs, the lapses, and the further promises of modern technics. We have observed the limitations the Western European imposed upon himself in order to create the machine and project it as a body outside his personal will: we have noted the limitations that the machine has imposed upon men through the historic accidents that accompanied its development. We have seen the machine arise out of the denial of the organic and the living, and we have in turn marked the reaction of the organic and the living upon the machine. This reaction has two forms. One of them, the use of mechanical means to return to the primitive, means a throwback to lower levels of thought and emotion which will ultimately lead to the destruction of the machine itself and the higher types of life that have gone into its conception. The other involves the rebuilding of the individual personality and the collective group, and the re-orientation of all forms of thought and social activity toward life: this second reaction promises to transform the nature and function of our mechanical environment and to lay wider and firmer and safer foundations for human society at large. The issue is not decided: the results are not certain: and where in the present chapter I have used the prophetic form I have not been blind to the fact that while all the tendencies and movements I have pointed to are real, they are still far from being supreme: so when I have said "it will" I have meant "we must."

In discussing the modern technics, we have advanced as far as seems possible in considering mechanical civilization as an isolated system: the next step toward re-orienting our technics consists in bringing it more completely into harmony with the new cultural and regional and societal and personal patterns we have co-ordinately begun to develop. It would be a gross mistake to seek wholly within the field of technics for an answer to all the problems that have been raised by technics. For the instrument only in part determines the character of the symphony or the response of the audience: the composer and the musicians and the audience have also to be considered.

What shall we say of the music that has so far been produced? Looking backward on the history of modern technics, one notes that from the tenth century onward the instruments have been scraping and tuning. One by one, before the lights were up, new members had joined the orchestra, and were straining to read the score. By the seventeenth century the fiddles and the wood-wind had assembled, and they played in their shrill high notes the prelude to the great opera of mechanical science and invention. In the eighteenth century the brasses joined the orchestra, and the opening chorus, with the metals predominating over the wood, rang through every hall and gallery of the Western World. Finally, in the nineteenth century, the human voice itself, hitherto subdued and silent, was timidly sounded through the systematic dissonances of the score, at the very moment that imposing instruments of percussion were being introduced. Have we heard the complete work? Far from it. All that has happened up to now has been little more than a rehearsal, and at last, having recognized the importance of the singers and the chorus, we will have to score the music differently, subduing the insistent brasses and the kettle-drums and giving more prominence to the violins and the voices. But if this turns out to be so, our task is even more difficult: for we will have to re-write the music in the act of playing it, and change the leader and re-group the orchestra at the very moment that we are re-casting the most important passages. Impossible? No: for however far modern science and technics have fallen short of their inherent possibilities, they have taught mankind at least one lesson: Nothing is impossible.